Make It Plain

MAKE IT
PLAIN

• • •

Standing Up and Speaking Out

VERNON E. JORDAN, JR.
with *Lee A. Daniels*

PUBLICAFFAIRS
New York

Page 209, lyrics to "Sweet, Sweet Spirit" by Doris Akers are courtesy of Manna Music, Inc. Copyright © 1962. Renewed 1990 by Manna Music, Inc., 35255 Brooten Road, Pacific City, OR 97135. All Rights Reserved. Used by Permission. (ASCAP)

Published in the United States by PublicAffairs™, a member of the Perseus Books Group.

Printed in the United States of America.

Book Design by Timm Bryson

Library of Congress Cataloging-in-Publication Data
Jordan, Vernon E. (Vernon Eulion), 1935–
    Make it plain : standing up and speaking out / Vernon E. Jordan, Jr. ; with Lee A. Daniels. — 1st ed.
        p. cm.
    Includes index.
    HC ISBN 978-1-58648-298-5
    PB ISBN 978-1-58648-775-1
    1. Jordan, Vernon E. (Vernon Eulion), 1935– 2. Jordan, Vernon E. (Vernon Eulion), 1935– Oratory. 3. Public speaking—Political aspects—United States. 4. African American orators—History. 5. African Americans—Biography. 6. African American political activists—Biography. 7. African American lawyers—Biography. 8. African Americans—Civil rights—History—20th century. 9. Civil rights movements—United States—History—20th century. 10. National Urban League—Biography. I. Title.
E185.97.J78A3 2008
323.092—dc22
[B]
2008032640

10 9 8 7 6 5 4 3 2 1

To Dan Davis

I have been very fortunate to be the beneficiary of the almost mystical affinity that in the best of circumstances develops between a speech maker and a speech writer. For thirty-five years, from 1971 to 2006, Dan Davis's expansive and precise thinking and facility with words has been invaluable in helping me flesh out my ideas and convey them crisply and elegantly. Our work together has exemplified the combination of trust, loyalty, and friendship that is as crucial as intelligence and skill at wordsmithing to the process of collaboration between speech writer and speech maker. We have discussed ideas and concepts frankly and without fear of the other taking offense. He has never objected to my being the final authority on the content of a speech, an authority I have fully exercised. But I've never doubted that at the end of my giving every speech we have crafted, he has always been the proudest person in the room for me. And I have continually realized and been more and more grateful for our professional relationship and our personal friendship.

This book's appearance indicates my good fortune in now having found the same essential common ground with another writer, Lee A. Daniels—like Dan Davis, an alumnus of the National Urban League.

●   ●   ●

CONTENTS

INTRODUCTION

January 30, 2008

I realized as this book began to take shape in 2007 that the
year encompassed two sets of events of profound relation
and resonance—one set echoing the past, the other dramati-
cally unfolding in the present. First, 2007 was a year of two
historic anniversaries: the sixtieth anniversary of Jackie
Robinson's breaking major league baseball's color barrier and
the fiftieth anniversary of the heroic stand the black community of Little Rock, Arkansas, undertook to integrate that
city's central high school. Those events demanded of their
participants what the centuries-long black freedom struggle
had always required: the determined pursuit of justice, unshakable courage against great odds, and what is often not re-
marked upon, an extraordinary patriotism and commitment
to the American ideal. They were part of the tapestry of
forces that ultimately compelled America to shed its overtly
racist laws and practices and expand opportunity across the
color line.

The bounty that expansion of opportunity has produced for all Americans showed itself at the highest level of our civic life in 2007 with the emergence of a black man and a white woman as the leading candidates for the presidential nomination of the Democratic Party. For me, celebrating within one year those two historic events of the past while contemplating the striking political possibilities of our present underscored something common to both: the critical power of words, often words delivered as speeches and in public advocacy, to move individuals and the nation. During the early and middle decades of the twentieth century, black Americans not only depended on the power of the word as a source of comfort and inspiration. They also effectively used it to compel white America to come to its moral senses and live up to Lincoln's great rhetorical description of the nation in the Gettysburg Address: "conceived in liberty and dedicated to the proposition that all men are created equal."

The speeches in this book, which begin with my becoming head of the National Urban League in 1971 and continue to the spring of 2008, were driven, above all, by my concern with black Americans' fundamental pursuit of the post–1960s era: to fuse the promise of the civil rights movement's legal and legislative victories with the actual lived experience of black Americans. They were meant to address the facts and circumstances of urgent issues roiling American society, supporting or rebutting the arguments of a particular moment. But, considering them both singly and in their totality now, they also do more than that. They outline earlier debates of some of the important issues Americans continue to grapple with today.

At this momentous point, as we turn from one presidency to another, the task facing all Americans today is, as it always has been, to make democracy work. In the 1960s, Roy Wilkins, the longtime head of the National Association for the Advancement of Colored People (NAACP); Whitney M. Young, Jr., my immediate predecessor as head of the National Urban League; Martin Luther King, Jr.; and many others understood that this goal was not going to be achieved merely by the enactment of the civil rights laws. They realized that the struggle to push democracy forward would have to continue, bolstered by new actors forging new paths that would connect black America more and more closely to the American mainstream.

In my work as an advocate in that journey during my years at the National Urban League and beyond, I have come to respect and love the craft of public speaking such that it has become an important part of my life. Early in my life, I decided I wanted to be an advocate for black America's quest to gain the full measure of American citizenship, and it was quite clear that required the ability to speak in a way that influenced people. If you are the state director of the NAACP in Georgia, as I was, and you can't get up in the pulpit and stir the congregation, you are not going to be successful. Most of all, these speeches offer lessons about and, I hope, inspiration for continued public advocacy for social justice.

The book's title comes from a long-held black American church tradition. In many black churches, when the preacher delivers the word in an especially compelling fashion, someone in the pews is likely to declare, "Make it plain, preacher, make it plain." That is what I have tried to do: *Make It Plain*.

My interest in public speaking came very early. It began in St. Paul African Methodist Episcopal Church, in Atlanta, with the children's Easter Sunday afternoon program. The children of the Sunday school were asked to give a memorized presentation, usually a combination of scripture and religious poetry on the theme of Easter. It was an important event in the life of the church and we were made to feel it was a significant step in our lives, too. Its fundamental purpose was to ground us in the church and in effect have us be advocates to the congregation about Easter.

The church was the bedrock of life in my public housing project. That's what you did Sunday mornings: You went to church. Both my parents were very involved in St. Paul. Its rituals and rhythms were interwoven with the Jordan family rituals and rhythms. So, as children, we memorized our speeches. We attended Easter practice several times a week, and then, come Easter Sunday afternoon at four o'clock, the congregation—parents and grandparents, and friends of parents and grandparents—assembled to hear us. All children got their applause. Even children who cried, stumbled, or remained silent out of fear, which happened often, were applauded. If you were good at delivery, to the applause would

be added murmurs of appreciation. *That's Sister Jordan's boy!*
That's Brother Hamilton's boy! Based on my Easter Sunday
performances, I competed in several citywide declamation
contests, representing St. Paul, where I often placed first.

I intuitively understood that speaking well was highly val-
ued. The very roots of the African Methodist Episcopal
(AME) Church and other black denominations sprang from
blacks' determination to be able to speak freely, passionately,
and persuasively. Blacks were not allowed to do that in most
of American society. Our voices were largely ignored when
they weren't completely stifled. But not in the black church.
There, you didn't have to have formal training or beg permission to speak. It was one of the few places where black people
could show their intelligence and demonstrate their eloquence, where they could not only discuss religion but relate
the lessons of scripture to the world around them. And often
those discussions focused on the rights black Americans were
entitled to but were being denied.

I grew up in Georgia in an era when the lives of black Americans were shadowed by limitation. The struggle to destroy
those limitations and restore civil rights was the central fact of
our lives. I understood this at an early age because many of the
leading figures in the community—teachers, preachers,
lawyers, doctors, ordinary working people—were involved in
civil rights work in some way. It often was the subject most
passionately discussed at the dinner table and at school, where
I learned about Negro History Week in the first grade, and at

public forums. The AME Church itself had been born in protest in 1787 in Philadelphia, when black worshippers, led by Richard Allen and Absalom Jones, refused to accept their second-class treatment by the white Methodist Episcopal Church. This consciousness permeated St. Paul. We were taught to look upon ourselves as descendants of Allen and Jones, who had an obligation to understand the AME Church's great tradition of practicing the social gospel—of using the lessons of the Bible to comment on broad social and economic conditions as well as the individual's relationship with God. It was that charge that most appealed to me, because it supported my early ambition to be a civil rights lawyer.

While I was aware of the injustice, I never felt intimidated by it. I never felt I needed to limit my aspirations. I observed all these strong black adults around me in church and in the community. And it was made clear to me from within my family, within St. Paul, and at Walker Street Elementary that there were expectations of me. I benefited from the black community's tradition of nurturing the talents of the young; that went on even where the restrictions against what blacks could aspire to were codified in thousands of laws. Because I had shown some talent, I was expected to do something with it. From the community and my family I had inherited an opportunity, and I believed I was in training, preparing myself for leadership in the future.

I had a rich diet of speakers to listen to at St. Paul. There were the Sunday morning sermons, of course, and because I sang in the St. Cecelia Choir, I also participated in the hour-long vesper services at five o'clock, where every fourth Sunday some outstanding person from the community would come to speak to us. The choir was personally underwritten by Dr. Richard A. Billings, our family physician, a prominent member of St. Paul, and a Lincoln Republican who voted against Franklin Delano Roosevelt. He mentored me from elementary school through my early career in the law. I paid very close attention to how these individuals—preachers and laypeople—would begin their speeches, how well they made the point or points of the speech, and how they finished up. I'd listen to them and I measured them and I had the audacity to grade them. Though young, I had my own sense of who had prepared well and who had not, who had been eloquent, who had shown a human touch that drew the audience to listen to them more attentively. I thought I understood whether and how the different parts of the sermons and speeches fit together. I understood that first, the speaker had to lay a good foundation, to give you his text and subject, to tell you what he was going to talk about. Then, in the middle part of the speech I looked for information and inspiration; even at a young age, I rejected volume and fireworks. Finally came the crescendo and the conclusion. How could I know all this as a young boy? It was all intuitive; I could feel it. What I understood then and what I understand now sixty years later is that if people have to listen to you, then you have a responsibility to give them something to listen to.

I also learned early where my own oratorical talents lay and where they did not. During Negro History Week one year at Walker Street Elementary, the teachers staged a program that had the students representing and speaking the words of accomplished black people. Of course, I wanted to play Joe Louis. But that part went to my friend Frank Hill; he went out on the stage to rousing applause from the students in the audience. My teachers had given me the role of William Grant Still, the conductor and composer. I walked out on the stage, declaring, "I am William Grant Still. I conduct symphonies that play Tchaikovsky and Brahms. . . ." It didn't go over well with the students; the reaction was tepid, at best. But my teachers saw more in me than I saw in myself. They saw I was better suited to play William Grant Still, that I had a voice and public personality made for the serious side of public speaking. My teachers sensed my ambition, and they pushed me in that direction. So, in school as well as in church, I became known as a speaker on serious subjects.

During my senior year in high school, a classmate, Ethel Wardell, and I entered the state Elks oratorical contest, held that year in Macon, Georgia, and we both won first place. That was a big deal—pictures in the *Atlanta Daily World*, the only daily black newspaper in the country, a notice on the bulletin boards at St. Paul, and congratulations from the congregation and people in the community.

In the second semester of my freshman year at DePauw University, I won the university-wide Margaret Noble Lee

Student Extemporaneous Speaking Contest. The concluding competition was held in the famed East College auditorium at Meharry Hall. I was one of the four finalists, drawn from more than 100 entrants. It was my luck to draw the shortest straw, making me the last to speak. The hall was filled to capacity and the audience, except for me and three of the other four black students at DePauw, was all white. I was confident I would win, and I did. My topic was "the Negro in America." Some might think it odd that I chose to take on that topic in the early 1950s before an audience that was sure to be almost completely white. But it never occurred to me to be anxious about that. I was at DePauw—where I had chosen to go to college. I knew my audience. Also, because most of the whites there had no experience being friends with or even talking to any black person, the topic, though "foreign," was of great interest to them. And I think they had respect for me and my ability to speak out.

In February of my sophomore year, I won first place in the men's competition of the Indiana State Oratorical Contest over ten other finalists. It was the first time that a DePauw student had won since Andrew J. Beveridge, who later became a U.S. senator from Indiana, had captured first place in 1896. Later that spring, I gained third place in the interstate oratorical contest involving college students from Illinois, Kentucky, Michigan, Ohio, and Pennsylvania, as well as Indiana.

At DePauw I religiously read the current issues of *Vital Speeches*, which contained many of the important speeches of the day, evaluating them as I had the words of the ministers and laypeople at St. Paul. Later, during my decade-long tenure at the Urban League, *Vital Speeches* would reprint several of my speeches. I also accepted every invitation from De-Pauw pre-theological students to speak at the rural white Methodist churches around Indiana they pastored for their "race relations day" exercises. It was a challenging experience. Often, I was the first black person many of these people had ever met, and white children would rub my skin and look at their hands to see if the color had come off. There was a great curiosity about black people and the issue of race. The audiences were always attentive and inquisitive, but I'm sure, not always in agreement with what I said. In some ways, it prepared me for the experience of the early 1970s when I began to serve on corporate boards and speak to gatherings of whites who had little contact with black people: There was the same profound curiosity and, in some instances, scarcely hidden hostility. All of these experiences at DePauw persuaded me that whatever I was going to do in life, public speaking was going to be a significant part of it.

Among the many reasons law school at Howard University was a wonderful experience was the Andrew Rankin Memorial Chapel, the university's church. During my three years at the law school, I almost never missed a Sunday service because Rankin Chapel hosted some of the greatest black preachers of the day—Vernon Johns, Benjamin E. Mays, Samuel D. Proctor, Gardner C. Taylor, Martin Luther King,

Jr., and the like. Vernon Johns, who had preceded King as pastor of the Dexter Avenue Baptist Church in Montgomery, Alabama, preached one Sunday on the subject, "The Vindication of the Human Experience." He began with a discussion of the graveyard poets, those eighteenth-century English poets whose work was suffused with a preoccupation with death, and ended with an interpretation of Melville's *Moby Dick*. When Vernon Johns preached, you could almost see the tumult of the scene—the roiling of the ocean, Ahab, harpoon in hand in the rowboat, ready to strike at the great white whale, Moby Dick's malevolent eye. Such verbal portraiture made the sermon all the more memorable because it was an emotional as well as an intellectual experience. Over the last ten years, I have been privileged to speak at Rankin Chapel, where laywomen and laymen are often invited as guest speakers.

When I returned home to practice law, I was invited to be "Youth Day" speaker and "Men's Day" speaker at various churches in Atlanta—great experience for a lawyer in the embryonic stages of his career, and it helped in the law practice. Giving those speeches was like an internship, a rehearsal for what was to come. Each time I spoke, it was a learning experience.

One of the most memorable was when, as field secretary for the NAACP in Georgia, I attended the convention of the Southern Christian Leadership Conference (SCLC) in the fall of 1962 in Richmond, Virginia. Martin Luther King had formed the SCLC as a coalition of ministers to expand and strengthen the nonviolent movement throughout the South, and the group's conferences were infused with the mix of social-gospel activism and great oratory that characterized the movement as a whole. The conference was held in the gymnasium of Virginia Union University, the historically black institution. Adam Clayton Powell, Jr., the Harlem congressman and pastor of the famed Abyssinian Baptist Church, was being given SCLC's Rosa Parks Award, so there was a huge crowd present for the event and it produced an extraordinary night of speech making. Powell was to receive the award after several of the leading ministers in the SCLC—among them Fred Shuttlesworth, C. K. Steele, C. T. Vivian, Ralph David Abernathy, Wyatt Tee Walker, and Andrew Young—spoke briefly, separated by musical interludes. Then, Adam was to say a few words, and Martin would end the program with brief remarks. I don't remember the exact order of the speakers. What I do remember is that with each succeeding speaker, the rhetoric became more pointed, the preaching more powerful, and the audience more excited. It quickly became clear to all that something special was taking place. It hadn't been set up to become a "preaching contest," but that collection of orators, with such knowledge and facility with language, produced one. Adam, who was a great preacher, just blew the top off the place. It took all of Martin's rhetorical skill and emotional power to win back the audience. For me, that evening exemplified the orator's duty:

coming prepared to do one's best but also being able to respond to the emotion of the moment to inspire as well as educate those listening to you.

That lesson was driven home to me by an experience I had soon afterward that, in terms of trappings and glamour, was very far from the SCLC conference. I was invited to give the Emancipation Proclamation Day Speech on New Year's Day to the Telfair County (Georgia) NAACP by its president, Alex Horne. I knew that Emancipation Proclamation Day programs in Atlanta were a very big deal. I wanted to do my best for Alex Horne, who also happened to be the foreman of Herman Talmadge's farm in McRae, Georgia, about a three-hour drive south from Atlanta.

I wrote my speech and left Atlanta on New Year's Eve night to begin the long drive to McRae. I first drove to Macon, eighty miles away. I rented a room at the colored motel there for $5.15, slept for a while, then got up and continued on the seventy-five additional miles to McRae. I arrived at the Horne household, where Mrs. Horne had prepared a great meal. Mr. Horne proudly showed me the printed program for the Emancipation Day activities. It was very elaborate, with the participation of several preachers, church choirs, and numerous laypeople. It was all due to begin at seven o'clock that evening.

When we got to the church, fewer than ten people were there. Alex and I were the only people listed on the program who were present. Not one preacher. Not one choir. Not one youth group. As a courtesy, they took up a collection to pay my expenses. It could not even pay for the cost of the gasoline. The church was cold because its small stove that sat beside the pews wasn't working. I had to speak in my overcoat. But I spoke to those eight or nine people as if they were 800 or 900. I gave them everything I had because they had come to hear me, and it was my responsibility not to disappoint them. That experience brought home to me in the most poignant way that the importance of a speech ultimately lies not in whether it's delivered before an overflow audience but that it be enriching for however many people are there. That's all the speaker can do. That's what the audience deserves. Since that moment, I have tried not to take any audience for granted, whether it consists of hundreds of people or just a few. That commitment has been the foundation of every speech I've ever made. I always think of my experience with Alex Horne and those eight or nine people as "bread cast upon the waters."

In 1956, Martin Luther King, Jr., whom the Montgomery Bus Boycott had just thrust into the public spotlight, delivered the Emancipation Proclamation Day Speech for the Atlanta NAACP at big Bethel AME Church. In many black communities before the great civil rights victories of the mid–1960s, Emancipation Day was a profoundly important event, which encompassed within its ceremonies the whole of the black experience in America: the travails of slavery and the battle over abolition, the bitter betrayal of Reconstruction, and the purposeful determination that lost rights should be regained. The 1956 speech was the first time I heard King put into words some of the sentiments and phrases that the world would ultimately come to hear in the "I have a dream" speech he gave in 1963 at the Lincoln Memorial. In 1956 it was, like so much of the black oratory of the time—whether exclusively scriptural or focused on civil rights—a work in progress. Words and phrases were tested on the audience, and eliminated or revised and refined, depending on audience reaction and the speaker's own sense of what needed to be said. Walking out of the church that day, I remember saying to my father, "Daddy, I'm going to make that speech one day." Ten years later, in 1966, I did give the Emancipation Proclamation Day Speech before the Atlanta NAACP, with my family in attendance along with many of the men and women whose civil rights work I had admired for so many years. Five of my dearest mentors were in the audience, nervous and proud, because they knew it was a big moment for me: Leslie Dunbar, the executive director of the Southern Regional Council; Ruby Hurley, southeast regional director of the NAACP and my direct boss; and three great civil rights lawyers, Wiley A. Branton, Sr., my law partner and my predecessor as head of the Voter Education Project; Donald L. Hollowell, who hired me right out of law school; and A. T. Walden, my childhood hero, who for many years had been the most prominent black lawyer and civil rights advocate in Atlanta. He was old then and so physically weakened that he had to wear braces on his legs. But when I finished my speech, Walden, who had been sitting in the pulpit behind me, stood up, hobbled over to me, and said, "Son, you hit a home run."

I knew then I was on my way.

URBAN LEAGUE BEGINNINGS

1971

The tragic drowning in March 1971 of Whitney M. Young, Jr., the executive director of the National Urban League, stunned the civil rights community, black America, and those white Americans who knew him as a dynamic, positive force for America. Whitney had been the league's executive director for a decade. His combining the organization's traditional commitment to social-service work with a substantive, highly visible involvement in the civil rights struggles of the 1960s had propelled it and him to the front ranks of America's black leadership.

And then, suddenly, he was gone.

Whitney's death generated a profound unease among black Americans, and not only because it meant the loss of another "soldier in the army" who had manned the front lines of the black freedom struggle. To many, it seemed another dramatic indication—the latest of a series of tragic deaths of notable public figures since the assassination of President John F. Kennedy—that something had gone terribly wrong in the American society of the late 1960s and early 1970s. The turbulence of those years was relentless: the shadow cast by the polarization over the war in Southeast Asia, the youth revolt on college campuses, the emergence of a more assertive black militancy and white resistance to it. For black Americans in particular, Whitney's death seemed to underscore the point he and others had been asserting for years: that the welcome destruction of the most obvious barriers of racial discrimination would inaugurate a new and challenging phase of blacks' quest to assume their rightful place in American society.

Whitney knew that the 1970s would require strategies to eliminate more subtle but still powerful barriers to black advancement that were less overtly dramatic than marches and sit-ins but no less important. Fashioning and implementing those new strategies was the task I took on when, less than three months after Whitney's death, I was chosen to be his successor. I was the more honored at having been chosen because Whitney and I had been friends through the 1960s, and that relationship had deepened when I became head of the United Negro College Fund in 1970. We began to see each other more frequently, in part because both our organizations' national offices were headquartered in Manhattan, housed in the office building we jointly owned. Several years earlier, Whitney had asked me to be his deputy before he withdrew the offer because, he told me, he believed I had the ability to head the organization myself and he wasn't intending to leave the Urban League anytime soon. When he learned that I was under consideration for the United Negro College Fund, he urged me to take the job. And when I did, he welcomed me to New York City, counseled me on the mores of the city's business and activist community, and made sure I met many of his own friends and supporters. His counsel and confidence in me were invaluable.

Succeeding my friend and mentor at the Urban League was a daunting responsibility. It added even more drama to the anticipation of my first speech as executive director at the organization's 1971 annual conference in Detroit. The speech was to prove me a worthy successor to Whitney.

The speech, scheduled for the conference's gala dinner on its final evening, was my coming-out party. Even though I had been involved in civil rights work for nearly a decade, I was unknown to the Urban League family. There was great curiosity and many questions, in part because I was not a professional social worker. All of my predecessors—the four previous Urban League executive directors, including Whitney—had been certified social workers, and the Urban League had always emphasized its social-service capability. So in giving this speech, I was on trial, like a preacher giving his first sermon. But I was prepared.

Sitting on the dais in Detroit's cavernous Cobo Hall, awaiting my turn to speak, I felt an invigorating tension, the kind of tension that makes you eager to get to the task at hand. But there was also apprehension among some members of the board and the staff. They were curious: would the new guy measure up?

That anxiety was underscored by my having to follow as a speaker Ossie Davis, the great actor, who along with his wife, Ruby Dee, was greatly admired throughout black America. Speaking in his well-known, mellifluous bass, Ossie welcomed me to the Urban League, pronouncing my last name as "Juurdan."

I saw an opening.

When I rose to speak, I thanked Ossie for his kind words, paused a moment, and then said to the audience: "Ossie and I are both from Georgia. But he's from Waycross, Ware County, in southern Georgia. I'm a city boy, from Atlanta. Up there, we pronounce my last name as "Jordan, not Juurdan!" And then, laughing, I turned to Ossie and said, "Got it?"

He laughed along with the rest of the audience. That seemed to break the tension, and I launched into my speech.

But even after Detroit, I fully expected that the testing of my leadership capacity from within the organization would continue, and it did.

One of the most memorable occasions occurred a year or so later when I was invited to speak at Harlem's Abyssinian Baptist Church during its Sunday service by its then pastor, Samuel Dewitt Proctor, a distinguished preacher and theologian. It was a high honor indeed to be invited to such a historic church, where both Adam Clayton Powell, Sr., and Adam Clayton Powell, Jr., had pastored for many years. But Livingston Wingate, the head of our New York affiliate, the

New York Urban League, whose headquarters were in Harlem, too, was not happy about my invitation. He was worried, he told me forcefully during a telephone call, that I wasn't up to the rhetorical challenge of speaking from Abyssinian's pulpit. "Abyssinian's congregation has heard the best orators. I don't want you to embarrass me," he said, ordering me to "cancel it."

I shot back: "Wingate, no. I've been invited to speak and I'm going to speak."

At Abyssinian, I got up and said, "I know I stand on hallowed ground, for my feet are planted where Adam Clayton Powell, Sr., and Adam Clayton Powell, Jr., stood for so many years. And as I stand here where they stood, I hear both of them saying to me from yonder in the halls of immortality and eternity, 'Son, make yourself at home.'" And a lady sitting in the front part of the church, her pronunciation of the word "help" reflecting deep Southern roots, bellowed out for all to hear, "Hope him, Lord, hope him."

To his everlasting credit, after the speech, Wingate walked up to me with a remorseful look on his face, extended his hand, and said, "I'm sorry. That was wonderful. I didn't think you had it in you."

I had realized from the moment I accepted the job that such doubts made it imperative for me to clearly define right away what the Urban League's mission was and would be during my tenure: an organization that was result- and issue-oriented, a forceful advocate for the cause of social justice, and a "bridge" for racial understanding. I needed to unmistakably fix our mission because whenever there's a change in leadership, people worry about what the new leader will do with the legacy of the institution and with its future. That was especially the case then because of the trauma Whitney's death had provoked.

Whitney had forged a creative partnership with President Richard Nixon and his administration—just as he had done with the administration of Lyndon Johnson—in a way that was precedent-setting for any black organization. Whitney understood that in the new environment of the late 1960s, black America needed to be able to draw on the resources of the federal government no matter which party was in power. The civil rights movement had compelled the national government to reconstruct the legal foundation of blacks' rights as citizens. Now, it had to use its power to help blacks gain the material resources and political muscle to bring those newly won rights to life and make blacks' pursuit of equality more than an empty rhetorical notion.

Shortly after I was chosen as Whitney's successor in June 1971, President Nixon invited me to the White House. I said to Nixon, "one thing you have to understand, Mr. President, is that, like Whitney, I'm going to call it as I see it, and some of it you won't like." He said, "I get it." At the end of our discussion, Nixon assigned John Ehrlichman, his assistant for domestic affairs, as my liaison to the White House. Soon, Ehrlichman and I began playing tennis on the White House tennis courts from time to time before our formal meetings. That resulted in some criticism of me within and outside the League.

I kept my word to the president, and we kept the "partnership" intact—even after the administration tested me.

One day at the league's offices, Enid Baird, my executive assistant, who in her forty years at the league had held the same duties with Lester Granger and Whitney, buzzed me on the intercom and announced that Leonard Garment, special White House counsel, had unexpectedly showed up. After we exchanged pleasantries, I said, "Leonard, this is an unexpected visit"—which he acknowledged. Then he laid out on my coffee table sheets with details of all of the grants the Urban League had from the federal government. A moment later, he laid out several newspaper clippings with statements I had made criticizing the president and some of his policies. He said: "You have to choose."

I told him: "I do not have to choose. The administration has to choose whether, in light of these news clippings, you're going to continue to do the right thing about the Urban League." We never lost federal support under Nixon.

Some blacks, even at the Urban League, criticized the relationship the league had with the administration. In 1973, after *Newsweek* magazine wrote a cover story entitled, "Whatever Happened to Black America?" that discussed my playing tennis with Ehrlichman, an Urban League employee approached me one morning in the elevator, wearing a dashiki, jeans, and Italian loafers. He said, "Mr. Jordan, you can't be my leader playing tennis on the White House lawn with John Ehrlichman."

"Which federal program are you on?" I asked. "I'm on the LEAP program." The Labor Education Advancement Program, funded by the Department of Labor, was our largest source of federal funds. I asked, "How much do you make?" He said, "$27,000," a salary which at that time put one firmly in the middle class. I said, "You know what? I'm down there playing tennis with John Ehrlichman so that you can be a $27,000 militant giving me hell about it." In 1981, the Reagan administration announced cutbacks to numerous federal programs, including LEAP. Based on the Reagan cutbacks, I had to make cutbacks at the league, and one of the individuals cut was the same staffer. Now, threatened with a layoff, he had one question on a visit to my office: "Mr. Jordan, can you get a tennis game at the White House?"

Contrary to conservative propaganda, the civil rights forces always recognized the importance of blacks' economic empowerment. The overarching slogan of the 1963 March on Washington was "For Jobs and Freedom." The speech Whitney gave there just before Martin Luther King, Jr., spoke focused on the need to improve blacks' economic opportunities. And during the last three years of his life, King himself focused his energies primarily on economic matters, culminating in his plans for the Poor People's March on Washington of 1968 and the sanitation workers' strike in Memphis that led him to his tragic destiny. Jobs and decent living standards for all. Those were always part of the civil rights agenda, because you have to have economic security in order to enjoy freedom. The "right to check in" to a hotel is useless if you don't have the wherewithal to check out. The agenda for the next phase of the freedom struggle, after the major legal victories, was about enabling blacks to get the wherewithal to check out. That was the challenge of the 1970s. To recognize that the black freedom movement was not over but had entered a new stage emphasizing economic justice was a very difficult concept for white America in general to acknowledge; and it was difficult for some in the black community to grasp as well. They didn't anticipate that when the walls of legal segregation came tumbling down, debris would be created. Expanding opportunity for jobs, improving black children's access to quality education, and the like, was in some ways as difficult to achieve as knocking the walls of legal segregation down. It's easier to deal with the Klan mentality when the guy is wearing a white robe. It's much more difficult to deal with it when the Klansman is wearing a three-piece suit. Head and heart haven't changed—only the uniform.

NATIONAL URBAN LEAGUE CONFERENCE
Detroit, Michigan
July 28, 1971

*T*he long hand of fate that so suddenly reached out one tragic afternoon in March took from our midst a leader of unparalleled courage, intellect, and integrity. Whitney Young is gone, and we are not likely to be soon blessed by the presence of one so great or so beloved.

My own personal loss of a friend and mentor is dwarfed by the magnitude of the loss to black people, and indeed to all Americans, of so inspiring a leader.

We can only overcome the hurt and the pain by recognizing that this man's legacy lives on in the principles for which he stood; it lives on in the strategies he formulated; and it lives on in the organization he led.

It is both a great honor and an immense burden to be asked to succeed this great man as executive director and to follow in the great tradition of George Edmund Haynes, Eugene Kinckle Jones, and Lester Granger, who is with us tonight. I accepted out of a deep sense of duty and responsibility to use whatever talents and abilities I have to help my black brothers and sisters to achieve full and complete equality, and to help my white brothers and sisters make this nation fulfill its ideals and obligations.

I embark on this new challenge with the determination to fulfill the hopes placed in me by the dedicated board, volunteers, and staff of this great movement. And as I embark on this new challenge, I humbly ask:

> Guide my feet, Lord, while I run this race,
> Hold my hand, Lord, while I run this race,
> 'Cause I don't want to run this race in vain.

It is my great fortune that the lonely duties of leadership will be shared by a movement so tested by time and proven by circumstance as the Urban League. No man can enter lightly upon the task of carrying on the mission to which Whitney Young brought such unique wisdom, effectiveness, and grace. At a time when black people, other minorities, and all poor people are afflicted with mounting unemployment and spiraling poverty, the men and women of the National Urban League are once again challenged to respond with the kind of pragmatic and creative programs the nation has come to expect from this great movement.

And as the nation looks to us for leadership, the Urban League movement faces the future united and unafraid. In ninety-nine cities spanning this vast land, the men and women of the Urban League will continue to march forward to build a better society for a better tomorrow. In the years ahead, we at the Urban League will continue to be: forceful advocates for the cause of black people and other minorities; a result-oriented, issue-oriented organization dedicated to serving the people; yes, we will continue to be a bridge between the races, forging unity and harmony in a land torn by strife and division.

It is imperative that in this noble task, we continue to seek allies where we find them, and continue to press for new ideas and new attitudes on the part of our nation's leadership. Like all Americans, we look to Washington, D.C., for the inspiration and the commitment to greatness that is the rightful heritage of this nation. And like many Americans, we have been disappointed.

Among the positive policies of the Nixon administration is its new program of creative partnership with the Urban League. This partnership of federal resources and Urban League expertise and credibility in the black community is a unique achievement that will aid in the solution of some of the problems faced by black people.

But it must be understood that the Urban League will continue to speak out forcefully on the issues. We will pursue our joint ventures with the government without abdicating our right to disagree when the occasion warrants disagreement. Like the tree planteth by the waters, the Urban League shall not be moved from its forthright commitment to articulate the needs and desires of the masses of black people who look to it for leadership.

We have been in business for over sixty years without appreciable federally financed programs in the past, and we have now undertaken those commitments not out of an institutional urge to expand, but out of a sense of dedication to the cause of all black and minority peoples, and by extension, to the cause of building a prouder and better America.

The record of the Nixon administration is one that combines elements of high purpose with an apparent neglect of the deepest needs of poor people and minority groups. "What the right hand giveth, the left hand taketh away" might be one way to describe some of the actions of our leaders in Washington.

A brief analysis of some major proposed social legislation serves to convince us of the mixed attitudes shown by the Democrats and Republicans and by the government.

The proposals for welfare *reform*, for example, represent the first major overhaul of the rotting welfare system since its establishment. For the first time, an administration has proposed a federally guaranteed income below which no family may fall. For the first time, the pressing needs of the vast armies of the working poor have been recognized in welfare legislation. For the first time, federal assistance will be available to unemployed fathers living at home with dependent children. We acknowledge that such proposals are historic ones that reflect the needs of the poor. Thus giveth the right hand!

But the left hand also taketh away! The proposals stop short of the necessary federal takeover of the entire welfare system. The basic federal payment levels are set far too low, less, in fact, than those now provided by forty-five states and the District of Columbia in cash and food stamps and less than twenty-two states now pay in cash alone. There are no provisions that would prevent states from cutting their own supplementary payments, with the result that millions of recipients may actually receive less than they are now getting. Provisions for work are both punitive and inadequate in the absence of sufficient day care centers, employment opportunities, and minimum wage standards.

Thus, an apparent major step forward shrinks back timidly from the historic greatness that could have been grasped. And instead of that final end of poverty amid affluence that might have been, we have a proposal from the Nixon administration that places yet another Band-Aid on the bleeding wounds of a nation crying out for major surgery.

Revenue sharing is another instance of political expedience triumphing over the desperate needs of urban centers that teeter on the brink of bankruptcy. The concept of providing federal funds to the cities is one that few could argue with, and it is to the credit of this administration that it has taken this step to relieve the groaning budgets of local governments. Thus giveth the right hand!

But black people remain rightfully suspicious of a plan that would provide large sums of money to towns and suburbs that exclude them and to localities that have not felt the hot breath of the pressures of poverty and urban decay. Black people are rightly suspicious of the diversion of funds from grants-in-aid programs regulated by the federal government in favor of relatively unrestricted grants to local governments with a long history of discrimination and callousness towards the poor and the black. And we are hardly reassured when, at a time that poor people are subject to regressive income and sales taxes, white homeowners are told that enactment of revenue sharing will result in lower property taxes. Thus then the left hand taketh away!

Housing is yet another major area of disappointment. The recent statement of federal housing policy, proclaiming federal disapproval of overt racial discrimination while tolerating economic discrimination, is a blow to all who know that it is only through equal access to decent housing and to the schools and amenities of the suburbs that black people can get their fair share of the shelter, education, and jobs in this changing society. The government's refusal to act against the implicit discriminatory effects of economic and zoning barriers delivers a cruel, crushing blow to all who need decent housing and to all who believe in an open society.

This pattern of one step forward, matched by another step back, extends to other aspects of American life affecting black citizens. Sickle-cell anemia is the target of a major federal program, as it should be. Cancer, a major killer, is the subject of an unparalleled national health effort with a specially created agency dispensing huge amounts of funds. But lead-based paint poisoning, a major health hazard in the ghetto, is totally neglected by both the administration and the Congress, although a mere $30 million can eradicate a menace that affects 400,000 children, permanently damages 6,000–8,000, and kills 200 annually. The government currently spends as much to deal with this dread killer as it does to combat gypsy moths and fire ants!

The record of ambiguity extends to the operating arms of the government, as well. Some cabinet departments have clearly demonstrated concern for black and poor citizens, while others have failed to respond to black demands for justice and have not fulfilled their legal obligations to take strong and affirmative action to enforce civil rights laws. It was not the intent of these laws to languish in dusty books, and it is not the intent of black people to allow their hard-won rights to be ignored.

But also, black people are concerned, too, at the way in which minor figures in Washington, endowed with only symbolic powers, have gratuitously insulted their leadership and, by implication, all black people. To mistake the legitimate and just demands of an oppressed people as "complaining and carping" is to betray an insensitivity and callousness unworthy of high office.

Must we, at this late date and after so many years of hardship and sufferings, have to remind the administration and the Congress of those wise words of Frederick Douglass, who said:

We must either have all the rights of American citizens, or
we must be exterminated, for we can never again be slaves;
nor can we cease to trouble the American people while any
right enjoyed by others is denied or withheld from us.

And so, in viewing this mixed record of the administration, we
ask it to bring forth from those clouds of ambiguity the bright
rays of clarity; we ask it to make its positive achievement a base
from which to launch a total commitment, with massive resources, for an end to poverty and racism in the land. We ask it to
turn our doubts into belief, and to provide that moral leadership
the poet speaks of when he says:

> One day posterity will remember
> This strange area, these strange times,
> When honesty was called courage.

As the president of the United States prepares for this historic
journey to China, we of the Urban League movement ask him to
make a spiritual pilgrimage to Black America; to demonstrate his
concern with the hungry children of the urban ghettos and the
rural farmlands as he is demonstrating his concern with the
strategies of world politics.

Such leadership will be needed in the trying days ahead, in
these days whose realities have moved beyond those of civil
rights, for it must be understood that the civil rights movement
of the sixties was a movement dedicated to obtaining, conferring,

and defining rights of black people, rights long enjoyed by the white majority. Our protests and demonstrations led to court decisions, congressional legislation, and executive orders, affirming new rights of black people.

But the effective use of those rights was relatively limited to those who, through their educational and economic backgrounds, could take advantage of the new opportunities. The man mired in poverty and hunger could not care less that the doors of the plush downtown hotel were now open to him or that he, too, could now buy a $50,000 house in a white neighborhood. Most of these newly won rights did nothing to help him pay his rent or put milk in his babies' stomachs.

What is happening in the black community in the 1970s is that the achievement gap among black people is widening, not lessening. The ranks of those who are using new opportunities to get better jobs and homes and schooling is increasing. But at the same time, the ranks of poor people alienated from the mainstream is swelling at an alarming rate.

So we are now charged to consolidate and implement the rights torn so bitterly from a reluctant nation in the 1960s, and to bring about the economic empowerment of black people in the decade ahead. It is the achievement of such economic empowerment that must be a major goal of the Urban League in the seventies. The task of the seventies, then, is to effect that social revolution long promised and long withheld—to restructure our economy and income distribution so that there are jobs and decent living standards for all.

This is a challenge to national leadership in all sectors, government, labor, business, and agencies such as ours. It means that the Urban League must be flexible and pragmatic, and that we must adjust our programs to the very real needs of the people. Our broad range of programs is indispensable to the millions of black people who look to us for help, but we must also be prepared to meet new needs as they develop.

As we examine the structure and the programs of the Urban League, and as we look at the activities this week and the results of our conference, we realize that the Urban League is a flexible, changing institution. We are aware of the need for change—not for the simple sake of change itself, but to meet the new demands placed upon us by our constituency. Indeed, as the poet tells us:

> New occasions teach new duties,
> Time makes ancient good uncouth.

Therefore, in my term of office, in addition to the present and planned Urban League programs, I hope to initiate new programs in several areas of major concern to the black community.

Voter registration in the North is one such area. Black Power will remain just a shout and a cry unless it is channeled into constructive efforts to bring about black political power and to influence the established institutions of American politics. Political power is more than electing a black mayor long after a city's tax base has eroded and the city's stability has fled across its borders to the suburbs. Black political power is more than a vague desire to preside over the cold corpses of once great cities.

The power of black ballots can be seen in the South today, where hundreds of black people hold elective office and where white politicians can no longer ignore the needs of black voters. In addition to the noticeable improvement in diction forced upon many segregationist politicians, the black vote has put into the governors' mansions of several Deep South states men of pronounced progressive sympathies who are announcing the death of Jim Crow and who herald a new area in race relations for a new South.

Alabama, a state in which an attempt to vote meant a visit from the Klan's night riders just a short decade ago, now has 105 black elected officials, more than any other state in the union, with the exception of New York and Michigan.

So it is crucial that this example of Southern black political power be brought north, especially in the light of the impending national elections in 1972. Black citizens must use their numbers to gain their rightful place in the political "browning of America." Black office holders amount to only three-tenths of 1 percent of the 522,000 elected officials in this country. A constructive black presence in the city councils, legislatures, school and planning boards, and other instruments of the popular will is essential if black people are not to close this decade as disadvantaged as we began it.

So the Urban League will mount a major voter registration and education drive in selected Northern cities, with special emphasis on young people, who, until the passage of the Twenty-sixth Amendment this year, could die for their country but could not vote. Their frustrations and their energies, and those of their parents, will be harnessed to a constructive effort to make participatory democracy a reality.

Another area in which the Urban League will move in the coming months is that of drugs. Drug abuse has become a major national issue, but only after white middle-class kids became its victims. Black kids have been nodding in doorways for decades, and no one cared. The veins of black youth have been pierced by death-laden needles, and society showed massive indifference. But now that King Heroin stalks the hallways of suburban schools, the country is up in arms and demands action. National, state, and local governments cannot avoid their responsibility to mount full-scale war on drugs and the criminals who push them, as well as on those law-enforcement officials who look the other way and profit from them.

We in the Urban League will take measures to set up model prevention and education programs to help remove from the black community this cancerous growth that destroys its children and makes its streets unsafe.

The Urban League is also uniquely situated, through its wide network of affiliates and its record of professional expertise, to mount Action Research Teams on both the local and national levels, Action Research Teams that will bring the facts and the necessary interpretations of those facts to black people and their leadership.

Years ago, when black people were to be kept down, it was done by thugs putting on dirty old white sheets and burning a cross on a lawn or by hanging someone from a tree. Separate and unequal was the law of the land, given legislative and judicial sanction, and the most awesome barbarities were inflicted upon black people by a system structured for oppression.

But times change, and as civilization progresses, similar results are achieved in new ways—cleaner, more efficient, more technologically advanced. Now, complex plans are produced by economists, city planners, lawyers, and other so-called authorities of every stripe. And hidden deep in the entrails of the documents produced are implications that keep black people economically disadvantaged and powerless.

Issues once clear are now cloudy. The whole range of governmental relations is shrouded in complexities most people cannot fully understand. Proposals for new housing sites, road and rapid-transit construction, welfare regulations, employment policies, metropolitan government, school board actions, and a host of other issues affecting the black community are in need of solid, research-based interpretations. The Urban League Action Research Teams will be able to dig out those facts and provide the black community and black leadership with an understanding of the issues behind the issues that will lead to effective strategies and informed decisionmaking.

Another area in which we plan to move is that of corporate responsibility. For too long, black leaders have marched to corporate boardrooms in search of support and programmatic backing. We, at the Urban League, hope to reverse this flow, to bring the corporate boardrooms to the people and to the streets.

The time is long past when America's powerful business leaders can calmly sit in their well-appointed offices and listen to lectures about the sufferings of black people. The time is long past when business leaders can hire a handful of black workers and donate a few dollars to a community cause and consider their responsibility ended.

The survival of America's corporate giants is directly related to the depth of their response to the great social issues that affect the society in which they do business and from which they reap profits. To date, their response, when measured against the need, has been feeble. In part this may be because they have been walled off from the feel, the sight, and the smells of poverty. I hope that in the coming months we, at the Urban League, can inaugurate a program in which leading corporate executives will learn at first hand, from poor people and from ghetto residents themselves, what it is like to be poor and black in this America in 1971.

Our aim will be to increase their awareness of the problems and to touch their souls so that the immense power of the corporate community, and the limitless influence corporate leaders have on government policymakers, will be used, at long last, on behalf of the poor and the deprived.

By these actions, the Urban League can begin to bring an even greater measure of accomplishment and hope for black Americans, and to some degree at least, counter the crisis of spirit that shrouds the national soul and darkens its days. For America is currently going through a period of self-doubt and despair that is unique in its history. The contours of America's faith in itself have been worn away by the strains of a bitterly resented war, by the misunderstandings and suspicions of the different generations, and above all, by the perpetuation of racial discrimination that splits asunder all hope of unity and partnership.

The polls tell us the dismal story of this crisis of spirit. A Gallup poll taken earlier this year showed that nearly half the people fear "a real breakdown in this country." This widespread anxiety for the future is unparalleled in past polls. Earlier this month, the Roper Organization reported that nearly two-thirds of the American people believe that the nation has lost its proper sense of direction. In startling contrast to the traditional American optimism, less than a fourth of those polled felt that the country generally is going in the right direction.

Such polls are but harbingers of the deep malaise we can sense in going about this rich and unhappy land. That sense of belief and accomplishment, so long a key characteristic of the American spirit, is ebbing fast; the sustaining spirit that lifted America high is losing its power.

It is increasingly clear to me that to the extent that there is among the citizenry hope and faith in the American ideals, they are held by those who suffered most and benefited least. Black people today, for all our righteous anger and forceful dissent, still believe in the American Dream. We believe today as we once believed in the dungeons of slavery; we believe today as we once believed in the struggles of Reconstruction, and we held our faith through the dismal days of separation and segregation.

We believe because this is our land, too. And we must, in this year of doubt and confusion, remind a forgetting nation that this land is ours, too, that we have lived here since before the Pilgrims landed, and we are here to stay. This nation too often forgets that this land is sprinkled with our sweat, watered with our tears, and fertilized with our blood. It too often forgets that we helped build America's power and glory, that we dug taters, toted cotton, lifted bales, sank the canals, and laid the railroad tracks that linked ocean to ocean. We, too, sing "God Bless America"; we, too, sing: "O beautiful for spacious skies, for amber waves of grain." We, too, as black people, pledge allegiance to what that flag and what America is supposed to represent. We've died in America's every war, and black men are dying tonight in disproportionate numbers in the rice paddies in Indochina.

Yes, this land is our land and America will work for black people, or it will not work for anyone!

And so it is black people, who, by our belief in the ideals of American democracy, can help this nation to overcome its crisis of spirit and enter a new era of hope and fulfillment. The Urban League movement is a key instrumentality of this effort to make America work for all of its citizens. It is to the Urban League that black people and poor people turn for leadership and commitment. It is to the Urban League that, from the crevices of this nation's poverty-stricken ghettos, comes the plea: Is there no balm in Gilead? Is there no physician here?

The true meaning of the Urban League was seen on that terrible Tuesday in March, when Whitney Young rode down 125th Street for the last time. That long ribbon of a street was thronged by the people he served, the constituency he represented. They were all there—blacks, whites, Puerto Ricans, schoolchildren, welfare mothers, businessmen, dope addicts, hard hats, preachers, and pimps. A cross section of America. Some sang, some prayed, some stared in wonder and shock. Some raised clenched fists and others bore handwritten signs bidding their leader farewell. Each in his own way honored a man who shared the passion and the action of his time on their behalf.

And as much as that outpouring of emotion and love was a personal testament to Whitney, it was also a demonstration that bore witness to the impact of the organization he led, the instrumentality of his greatness—the National Urban League.

Those many thousands who waited patiently that day to honor a fallen hero, who turned in their grief and despair of the moment to an incredible testament of love and mourning, those people turn today to the Urban League movement. We leave this conference bolstered by their faith, their strength, and their power. We leave this conference steadfast and determined to reach a new higher pitch of effectiveness. And we leave this conference with a strength renewed in a cause just and a spirit righteous. And in leaving,

> Let us go, Let us do our work,
> Let us neither stumble nor falter,
> Let us mount up with wings as eagles,
> Let us run and not be weary,
> Let us walk and not faint.

NEW IDEAS FOR
THE NEW SOUTH

1976

The speech I gave to a joint assembly of the South Carolina State Legislature on March 10, 1976, was an extraordinary moment. In a sense, I felt as if I were standing on a bridge between the past and the future. South Carolina holds a special place in American history and in the history of the black freedom struggle. In the antebellum era, South Carolina's white citizenry had been among the most fervent defenders of Negro slavery and advocates for secession. It was the state where the first shots of the Civil War were fired at Fort Sumter. And white South Carolinians quickly undermined the state's post–Civil War democracy, establishing in its place a stultifying apartheid. Ninety years later, South Carolina produced one of the school desegregation cases—*Briggs v. Elliott*—that led to the U.S. Supreme Court's 1954 landmark ruling in *Brown v. Board of Education of Topeka*.

The previous evening, that history had rolled across my mind. Arriving in Columbia, the state capital, I was immediately surrounded by some of the most powerful symbols of the attitudes and actions that had once ruled the South. A room had been reserved for me in the hotel, directly across from the capitol grounds, named for Wade Hampton, the Confederate general and anti-Reconstruction governor and senator. The next morning, as I walked across Gervais Street toward the capitol building, the first statue I saw was that of John C. Calhoun, one of the principal architects of the antebellum secessionist fervor. The second statue I encountered paid homage to Pitchfork Ben Tillman, one of the most rabid of the South's post–Civil War demagogues.

And yet I also realized that those statues existed only as monuments of days gone by and of a culture whose brutal ideology had been defeated by history. As I spoke to the assembled representatives of the people of South Carolina, I knew I would be buoyed by the presence in the chamber's gallery of scores of black schoolchildren whom Majesta Simpkins, a stalwart freedom fighter from the South Carolina NAACP (National Association for the Advancement of Colored People), had ushered in to witness my speech. I was fully aware that the winds of change had been blowing across the state of South Carolina as strongly as anywhere else in the nation. My invitation, the first any Southern legislature had extended to the leader of a civil rights organization, was evidence of that. William B. Whitney and Hiram Spain, di-

rectors of the Urban League affiliates in Greenville and Columbia, South Carolina, respectively, had suggested the invitation to State Representative Theo Walker Mitchell, one of the
first blacks elected to the legislature after Congress had en-
acted the Voting Rights Act of 1965. Mitchell took the idea to
Rex Carter, the Speaker of the House, and he readily agreed.

Blacks' regaining the right to vote had fostered an expo-
nential increase in the number of black registered voters and
black elected officials in the states of the old Confederacy.
That, in turn, compelled white elected officials who clung to
the old attitudes to cling to them in private. In public they
had to produce benefits for their black constituents, too, if
they wanted to stay in office. More positively, the political
change set in motion by the civil rights victories brought into
both elective and appointive offices a new corps of white
politicians committed to serving the entire public of the
South. And the South as a whole reaped the benefit. Indeed,
in that spring of the nation's bicentennial year, the American
people were witnessing the first credible campaign for the
presidency by a white Southern politician—Jimmy Carter—
of the twentieth century.

These were some of the facts that enabled me to be invited to speak that day to the South Carolina State Legislature and be escorted to the dais by two black state senators
and three black state representatives, and by one white state
senator. Not every trace of past attitudes had disappeared.
Richard Riley was the only white legislator who had signed

up to be part of my escort committee that day. But it is worth noting that just two years later, Riley was elected to the first of his two terms as governor of South Carolina (and he later forged a distinguished record as secretary of education during President Clinton's two terms). In fact, I was very cordially welcomed both by the state legislators and later by Republican governor James B. Edwards during a reception at the governor's mansion. In any case, I had come to South Carolina not to dwell exclusively on the past. I had come to speak of the present that shadowed a nation still dispirited by the disgrace of Richard Nixon in 1974 and its ignominious retreat from Southeast Asia in 1975. There was a compelling need in America to address our common problems together, and my sense of it that day was that there were people in the legislature of the state of South Carolina who were willing to listen.

JOINT SESSION OF THE GENERAL
ASSEMBLY OF SOUTH CAROLINA
Columbia, South Carolina
March 10, 1976

I join you today in gratitude for your invitation, and deeply mindful of the historic nature of this occasion. My presence here is indeed symbolic of the giant strides toward maturity and toward interracial cooperation we have made here in the South.

Who among us would have thought a dozen years ago that a black civil rights leader would be invited to share with this distinguished body his views on the pressing issues of our times? Who among us, years ago, could have predicted that this General Assembly would include among its distinguished membership black political leaders? And who among us in that not-too-distant past could have foreseen the great changes in race relations that have taken place?

So, moved as I am by the personal honor bestowed upon me, I cannot but reflect on the symbolic nature of this event, and on the recognition it implies for the constructive work of the organization I represent, the National Urban League.

The National Urban League is a key institution in the black community, and in the white community as well. It provides vital community services, an advocacy voice for minority Americans, a bridge between the races, and is committed to the open, pluralistic, integrated society.

Among our 104 affiliates, I am proud to number twenty-five in the South, including the Urban Leagues of Columbia and Greenville, with whose great work I hope you are familiar. The leadership of those leagues is here today—Lincoln C. Jenkins, president, and Hiram Spain, executive director of the Columbia Urban League, and from Greenville, Joseph T. Allmon, president, and William B. Whitney, executive director. These two leagues have a combined budget of over $1 million, employ over 100 people of both races, and serve their communities with successful programs in jobs, training, counseling, education, child development, and a host of other key areas.

This year we celebrate America's bicentennial, the two-hundredth anniversary of our nation's independence. It is also an election year.

It is, then, a time uniquely situated for self-examination, for redefining what America is all about, and for dealing with the unfinished business of fulfilling the American Dream, the still-to-be-completed promise embodied in our Declaration of Independence that "all men are created equal, that they are endowed by their creator with certain inalienable rights, that among these are life, liberty, and the pursuit of happiness."

Those words shine like beacons through the ages, they have inspired men in far-off countries, as they have inspired our own people. They stand today as reminders that the barriers of race, of poverty, and of joblessness should not be tolerated in the birthplace of liberty and the fount of equality.

America's birthday celebration is tarnished because it occurs in a year of intolerably high unemployment, of rising poverty, and of continued national economic recession. Thus, our bicentennial must be the occasion not merely for self-congratulation but for a critical appraisal of what must be done to extend our national ideals to all of our citizens. The grim reality of unequal opportunity for many millions of Americans should inspire us to positive actions to reorder our national priorities and fulfill the aspirations of all of our people.

There are today in America over 24 million people officially classified as poor, and some estimates place the number at 40 million because the official poverty line has lagged behind rising prices.

There are today in America over 7 million people officially classified as unemployed, and if we add to them 5 million discouraged workers who have given up looking for nonexistent jobs, and over 3 million part-time workers who want full-time work, we find some 15 million people unemployed or subemployed. And that does not even include about 2 million people who work full-time for below-poverty-level wages.

Those are national statistics. Here in the South, the situation is even worse; the poverty rate, involuntary part-time work, and subemployment are all higher.

And both nationally and regionally, black people fare worse than do whites. Southern black unemployment is over double the white rate; a third of all black families are poor, and half of them do not receive a single cent from welfare; earnings of black workers average only about two-thirds that of whites; and in almost every measure of socioeconomic status, blacks lag behind whites, and in many instances, the gap is growing, not closing.

Just as a disproportionate number of Southern whites are poor and subemployed, so, too, do we find a disproportionate number of Southern blacks lagging behind their white neighbors.

Thus, Southerners have a strong stake in national policies that increase employment opportunities and reduce the shameful poverty that still stalks our land.

Despite the current popularity of optimistic predictions about the economy, it is clear that unemployment and poverty will continue to remain at unconscionably high levels. Administration spokesmen predict unemployment will still be at the 7-million level by year's end and full employment is now universally regarded as unattainable.

To accept this, however, is to accept continued joblessness for many millions of people who desperately want to work, white and black alike. To accept this is to doom those people and their children to marginal economic existence and to rob America of the full prosperity for all that she is capable of achieving. And to accept this is to doom ourselves to artificially lowered living standards and to federal budget deficits.

For every million people out of work, the government loses $16 billion in lost tax receipts and in unemployment benefits. This year alone, abnormally high unemployment rates cost our economy over $150 billion in lost economic growth; this year alone, the federal government will spend over $40 billion in unemployment compensation and in welfare costs, most of which would not be necessary if we had full employment.

If our nation had implemented a full employment policy twenty years ago, we would have produced in that time an extra $2 trillion worth of goods and services, and federal tax receipts would have gained some $500 billion.

Thus, we must ask whether we can afford *not* to have full employment.

I would hope that this distinguished body will go on record in support of a national full-employment policy that guarantees a decent job at a decent wage to all Americans able to work. I envision a three-pronged program to achieve this goal. It would include:

+ Incentives to private industry to recruit, train, and hire the jobless. The private sector can't do the job alone, but public policies that make it less attractive for a business to hire more workers compound the difficulty. Federal regulations, subsidies, and tax incentives should all be directed at increasing the private sector's ability to create jobs.

+ A second step would be for the federal government to create a public works program along the lines of the old WPA [Works Progress Administration] that helped sustain millions during the Depression of the 1930s. Those public works projects lined our country with roads, with bridges, with schoolhouses, and other public facilities still in use today. A similar program in the seventies would not only create jobs, but it would provide a new generation of vitally needed houses, transportation facilities, and other public works our nation needs.

+ Finally, a vastly expanded public-service employment program would help fill the pressing need for public services while assuring employment opportunities for millions of people. Some years ago a presidential commission determined that public-sector manpower needs in conservation, safety, education, and health could accommodate some 5 million new jobs, offering an opportunity to sharply improve necessary public services.

A national full-employment policy along the lines I have out-lined here would make unemployment a thing of the past, turn revenue-consumers into producers, generate tax income to pay for itself, and remove the curse of joblessness from the land.

A national full-employment policy, along with a national income-maintenance plan, would have its greatest impact right here in the South, and would go a long way towards bringing our region to economic parity with the rest of the country.

Such a policy would not, by itself, end poverty, for there would remain those who are unable to work, who are incapable of work-ing and thus in need of assistance that would enable them to maintain a decent living standard. The welfare system is supposed to do this, but its faults are too numerous to detail here. Everyone agrees that the welfare system is a mess, that it discourages work, penalizes the poor, and encourages dependency. It is an inconsis-tent patchwork of bureaucratic interference in people's lives, wildly varying benefit scales, and costly administrative charges.

But its worst fault is that it doesn't work. The welfare system for the poor is not nearly as efficient as the welfare system com-posed of tax loopholes and subsidies for the wealthy. That's why there is growing support for a welfare reform program that as-sures a livable minimum income while relieving state and local governments of the increasing burden of providing for the needs of the poor.

I believe the most efficient reform would be a universal refund-able credit income tax that would extend a basic annual grant, or tax credit, to all. That grant would be taxable income, so that the poor would keep all of it, the near-poor would keep some of it, and middle- and upper-income families would return it all in taxes.

This system would be financed by removal of most of today's tax deductions and loopholes and the imposition of a flat tax rate on all income. Such a system would limit subsidies to those in need, and not, as at present, to the better-off. It would supplement the incomes of working families who cannot make ends meet. And because the tax credit would be automatic and universal, it would bring big savings in administrative costs and reduce abuses so prevalent in the present system.

In fact, we have the beginnings of such a system today. Families whose incomes are below $4,000 get a cash payment from the IRS [Internal Revenue Service]. Those between $4,000 and $8,000 get lesser amounts.

The tax credit route to welfare reform has attracted increasing support, including key elements within the administration. Support for federal takeover of welfare has also mounted, with several governors urging such action. It is clear that some such reform will come sooner or later, and the national nature of the problem, the continuing economic crisis confronting low-income citizens, and the growing disenchantment with the present malfunctioning system all argue for sweeping reforms as soon as possible.

My proposals for a national full employment policy and for a universal refundable credit income tax are pro-work, pro-human dignity proposals. They would increase national productivity, stimulate the economy, end unemployment, and lessen poverty.

And they would go a long way toward removing the economic causes of racial antagonism.

It is too often forgotten that many more whites than blacks are jobless, are poor, and are receiving welfare. It is too often forgotten that while blacks suffer disproportionately higher rates of economic hardship, five times as many whites are jobless and twice as many are poor.

So these issues cannot be framed in racial terms; they cannot be seen solely as "black" issues. Just as more whites than blacks benefited from the social programs of the sixties, so, too, would more whites than blacks gain from full employment and from welfare reform.

And we should also remember that as our nation confronts an increasingly hostile world, a key element in our defense arsenal must be internal stability and economic growth. By healing the divisions within, we strengthen ourselves and increase our ability to lead our friends and inspire respect in our enemies. But there is another view that says we can't afford full employment programs, income maintenance programs, and other needed reforms. It is a view that argues that the federal government has become too big, and that it should retreat from social and economic intervention in our society.

This view, which I call "the new minimalism," counsels a planned withdrawal from national greatness that is subversive of the ideals of equality embedded in the Declaration of Independence. And the new minimalism is wrong in its facts.

For the fact is that the federal share in the economy has not risen at all. Between 1953 and 1973, the federal budget has held steady at about 20 percent of the gross national product. The slight rise since 1973 is directly attributable to recession-related costs of unemployment compensation and welfare. That federal debt that's supposed to be so high is only about 26 percent of the GNP; back in 1950, it was an astonishing 82 percent.

Obviously, the federal government can be more responsive to the needs of its citizens and the private sector; it can be more efficient and more productive. It needs to take a hard-nosed look at costs and keep them to the minimum necessary, while it also must take a hard-nosed look at national needs and supply them to the maximum extent necessary. Just fussing at bureaucrats and at Washington won't put people to work, nor will it take us out of the cycle of boom and bust that retards our progress.

Southerners must be especially wary of the new minimalism, for this region would be the prime beneficiary of federal job-creation programs and of federal income-maintenance programs. The economic gap between the South and the rest of the country remains, and we've got a stake in the federal responsibility to reduce that gap and to enlarge the potential of our society.

But there's another reason why Southerners must be suspicious of the new minimalism, and that is because it was largely the federal initiative toward securing civil rights that has led to the true emergence of a New South, and freed us from the institutionalized racial oppression that brought terrible harm to all Southerners—black and white.

Those civil rights laws that the new minimalists might cite as unwarranted federal intrusions actually provided the springboard

for the region's progress. The growth of its economy, the infusion
of industrial capital, and the establishment of job-producing new
industries by national and international corporations could never
have occurred if those corporations had to operate in the old environment of separate drinking fountains, separate public facilities, and separate labor force patterns.

Yes, the South has changed, the New South is a reality, not an
empty phrase, and there is a new dawn in the relations between
the races. Discrimination still exists. Old patterns still survive.
But I have faith that these are dying remnants of an old order
that could not survive the fresh winds of the twentieth century.

When Senator Thurmond supports Matthew Perry for the
Military Court of Appeals, you know there have been changes;
when Southern students go to Boston to counsel school bodies
on how to integrate, you know there have been changes. And
when a black civil rights worker from Georgia is invited to speak
to you today, you know there have been changes.

Many of the changes are directly related to black voting power
and to the black use of long-overdue constitutional rights. But
many also derive from sincerely changed attitudes on the part of
many people who, ten years ago, cried "never," and who cried "inter-
position," "nullification," "massive resistance," and "no, not one."
They have found it is easier to do right than to keep on doing
wrong.

But for all the very real changes, black people remain seriously
disadvantaged. It would be all too easy to become complacent, to
allow highly visible or cosmetic changes to obscure the real in-

equities in our society. So let us restrain our enthusiasm for the fact that the worst features of the Old South have departed and let us continue to work for fulfillment of the South's potential as a beacon for the rest of a nation torn by racial divisions and economic inequities.

It is the South, above all other regions, that can teach our fellow Americans of the futility of racism, the evils of economic exploitation, and the necessity for positive, constructive change. It is the South that can bring a humanizing influence to bear on the new technology and new industrial development. It is the South whose unique history can demonstrate to the rest of the nation the value of racial reconciliation and partnerships.

Whether the South will do this, or whether it will be content to become just another section, indistinguishable from the others, depends in large part upon its continued progress in race relations and upon its ability to include black people as full economic equals. It depends on what this assembly and others like it in the South do about issues at the state level that directly affect the well-being and the opportunities of black citizens. It depends on whether we come to recognize that black disadvantage is the result of special treatment for over 400 years, and that now, a new, positive kind of special treatment is needed to make up for the past.

Lyndon Johnson said it so well just a few weeks before he died: "To be black in a white society," he said, "is not to stand on level and equal ground. While the races may stand side by side, whites stand on history's mountain and blacks stand in history's hollow.

Until we overcome unequal history, we cannot overcome unequal opportunity."

Let us, then, strive to overcome the unequal history we have shared these four centuries. Let us, black and white, come together in friendship and mutual respect. Let us forge together a creative partnership that will make our state, our region, and our nation a light for all mankind. Let us be mindful of our obligations to a tortured past, a difficult present, and above all, to a brighter future. Let us have faith in ourselves, in our ability to transcend the divisions of race and class and together, to build a golden, promised land for blacks and whites in our Southland—a land of justice, decency, and true democracy.

Yes, let us have faith. Black people have that faith. It was faith that helped us survive the harsh past and led us to become the initiator, the cutting edge, the moral force that moved the South to change its ways and strive toward its potential for greatness.

Black people have that faith because this is our land, too. We have been in South Carolina since 1526—long before the Jamestown settlement or the Pilgrims of Plymouth Rock. The first American to fall before British bullets was a black runaway slave—Crispus Attucks. Five thousand black soldiers fought side by side with white soldiers in the Revolutionary Army that won our independence.

Yes, this America is our land; it is the land we love, the land we have sacrificed for, the land we believe in still. Our faith in our nation is boundless. It is a faith that laments the injustices of the past and the present but knows that the sleeping giant that is America, the great nation whose bounty and whose freedoms will one day be extended to all of its children, will awaken from its moral slumber and that black and white, together, we shall overcome.

BATTLING THE CALLOUSNESS
OF POLITICAL REALITY

1977

T he early to mid–1970s were a time of extraordinary
political ferment in black America. The Voting Rights
Act of 1965 had rapidly changed the political landscape of
both the South and the North, where blacks had won decid-
edly few elective offices until then. By 1976, blacks had been
elected mayor in such major cities as Cleveland, Atlanta, and
Gary, Indiana, and had tripled the total number of elective
offices they held to more than 1,400. The number of blacks in
Congress had quadrupled from four to sixteen, and, in the
person of Representative Shirley Chisholm of Brooklyn, a
black had in 1972 mounted a credible campaign for the Democratic Party nomination for president.

But along with the great and obvious benefits, there were
still lessons to be learned—a reality underscored by Jimmy
Carter's capturing the White House in 1976.

Jimmy Carter and I have been friends since his first campaign for governor of Georgia in 1966. In our very first

meeting in my offices at the Voter Education Project of the Southern Regional Council shortly after he had lost that race, I collected several of the educational materials on race the council produced, put them in a plain envelope, and suggested to Carter that he digest them in his quiet reading time in Plains. I'm confident that he did. What I most remember was his saying to me, "Pay no attention to what I say, but watch what I do." I kept that in mind throughout his winning campaign for the governorship in 1970. Although as a candidate for president he would draw the support of Andy Young, Daddy King, and Coretta Scott King, then, he had made a concerted appeal to white conservative voters and had toured the state with Alabama governor George C. Wallace, who remained a symbol of white resistance to black advancement. Then, in his inaugural address Carter delivered a thunderbolt:

> This is a time for truth and frankness . . . at the end of a long campaign, I believe I know our people as well as anyone. Based on this knowledge of Georgians north and south, rural and urban, liberal and conservative, I say to you quite frankly that the time for racial discrimination is over. . . . No poor, rural, weak, or black person should ever have to bear the additional burden of being deprived of the opportunity of an education, a job, or simple justice.

Later in his term as governor, he appointed Jesse Hill, Jr., president of the Atlanta Life Insurance Company, to the

State Board of Regents, which was an equally stunning breach of the old racial etiquette.

An even greater dimension of the benefit to America of the civil rights movement in general and the Voting Rights Act in particular showed itself in the presidential election of 1976. Amid the yearlong celebrations of the nation's bicentennial, black Americans overwhelmingly backed Carter in both the Democratic primaries and the general campaign. They made it clear they saw Carter as a leader of the New South: a white Southern politician who had forged common ground with black political and civic leaders on his state's pressing issues. Not even his famous gaffe seeming to support the "ethnic purity" of white residential neighborhoods could shake black voters' confidence in him. They understood that Jimmy Carter embodied the fact that the movement had not only enfranchised blacks, it had freed white Southerners, too. Among other things, the South's shedding of legalized discrimination was making it possible for national and international companies to locate plants and headquarters there, spurring needed economic development in cities and rural areas. The movement's successes had unchained the South's educational and cultural institutions from the grip of a calcified racist orthodoxy that had always stunted their intellectual growth. It had enabled the professional sports leagues to, finally, locate franchises in the sports-mad region and its now desegregated colleges and universities to maintain their fervent pursuit of athletic success. Politically speaking, all this meant that white Southern politicians could now realistically dream of occupying the White House.

Carter and his longtime aides, Hamilton Jordan and Jody Powell, crafted a masterful campaign strategy that propelled him from the margins of national political life to decisive victories against his Democratic primary opponents and President Gerald R. Ford in November. His calm demeanor on the campaign trail offered a sharp, welcome contrast to the, in their very different ways, outsized personalities of Presidents Johnson and Nixon. And unlike President Ford, Carter was not a Republican and had not pardoned Nixon for the constitutional crimes unearthed as a result of the Watergate scandal. These qualities and his seeming commitment to dispassionate decisionmaking promised relief to a nation battered by the turbulence of the preceding decade and a half.

But by the summer of 1977, six months into his presidency, when the Urban League convened in Washington for its annual conference, there was a clear sense of disappointment among much of the Democratic Party coalition that had voted Carter into office. They, and we, found the policies he had put forward markedly insufficient to attack poverty and the urban crisis. Pay no attention to what I say, but watch what I do. As governor, Carter had been true to the implicit promise of his words. But his seemingly diffident approach to the domestic crisis during his first months in office was deeply disappointing, given the support the black community

had given him and the expectation that he would be an advocate for our needs and aspirations. The severity of the crisis
was underscored that very month by an event that cast the
plight of the poor and the cities into the sharpest relief: the
massive blackout that struck New York City on the evening
of July 13 and the frenzy of looting that immediately erupted
in the city's poorest neighborhoods. Because the first six
months of any administration are when its priorities and patterns of governance are set, I knew it was crucial—both to
the president and for black America—that I speak out.

I did alert Carter's White House staff that I was going to
be sharply critical of administration policies. They ignored
my signal because, first, they didn't believe I would do it, and
second, they didn't think my words would have any impact.
Of course, the speech immediately drew significant notice
because it was coming from a major civil rights organization
and because it was coming from a fellow Georgian and
friend, and because the president was coming to speak to the
Urban League conference the very next day.

I criticized the president's policies with the same frank-
ness I had employed in describing what I saw as the flaws of
the policies of the Nixon and Ford administrations—and
the press covered the speech extensively. Carter was upset
with the criticism, as he made clear in a news conference and
in his own speech to the conference the next morning. That
intensified the coverage; and it prompted support of my criticisms not only by leaders of other civil rights groups and the

Congressional Black Caucus, but also by George Meany, the powerful head of the American Federation of Labor and Congress of Industrial Organizations (AFL-CIO). I took no pleasure in faulting Jimmy Carter's leadership; and my criticisms of his administration were attached to specific policy recommendations we at the Urban League believed would result in an effective anti-poverty program. But I had no doubt that both actions—criticizing the president, and suggesting how his policies could be improved for the good of the country—were part of the duties of leadership that I had to adhere to. Reacting to the speech, Carter used unfortunate language in calling me a demagogue. But we still maintained our friendship and I still had access to the White House. In fact, it prompted the Carter staff to call us more frequently to get our views on policies and actions they were contemplating.

Blacks' disappointment with the first actions of the Carter administration offered an important learning experience for a people who in mass terms had only recently been able to play the game of politics at the highest level of national life. The lesson was that it's not enough to cast one's ballot and then go home. We blacks, like other political blocs, had to develop the resources to continually apply sustained pressure to even our political allies so that, amid the political clash of competing interests, the issues we considered important would be their priorities as well. That was the callousness of political reality.

NATIONAL URBAN LEAGUE ANNUAL CONFERENCE
Washington, D.C.
July 24, 1977

O nce again we meet in our nation's capital. Once again, the National Urban League movement convenes to press the just demands of black citizens upon a newly installed national government.

It is well to recall that our last annual conference in this city was held while guns and bombs were bringing death and destruction in Vietnam, while high officials were covering up the Watergate scandal, and while a hostile administration was trying to roll back the gains made by black citizens.

Today, the atmosphere is radically different. The guns of war are silent. Corruption, cover-up, and the abuse of power have gone out of style. And a new administration is openly consulting citizens' groups in policy formulation, while giving new recognition to the sanctity of human rights.

In the White House, we have a president whose devotion to equal opportunity is unquestioned. Long before he became our president, Jimmy Carter was our friend. Long before he was even a candidate for the presidency, Governor Jimmy Carter of Georgia came to Urban League meetings proudly wearing our equality pin in his lapel. And now, as president of the United States, he will honor us by coming to speak at this National Urban League Annual Conference.

In the short time he has been president, Mr. Carter has impressed us with his personal style. He has helped heal the wounds of a divided nation by deflating the "imperial presidency," by reaching out to his fellow citizens, and by backing an amnesty program that seeks to put the horrors of Vietnam behind us.

President Carter has touched us deeply by stressing the importance of human rights in a world that commonly flaunts those precious innate rights, and this is a cause that speaks to our hearts with a special significance.

President Carter has won our admiration by pursuing an African policy that, for the first time in our history, treats the aspirations of Black Africa with respect and encouragement.

These, and other accomplishments of the new administration have won our support. The style of openness and access to decisionmakers has breathed new life into our form of government. The symbolic acts of the administration have put us back in touch with our leaders.

Why then, do we convene in Washington with troubled minds and heavy hearts? Why then, are black people disenchanted with the administration they elected? And why do so many black people feel that their hopes and their needs have been betrayed?

The sad fact is that the list of what the administration has *not* done far exceeds its list of accomplishments. The sad fact is that the administration is not living up to the First Commandment of politics—to help those who helped you.

The administration has formulated a new foreign policy, a new defense policy, and a new energy policy. But it has *not* adequately addressed itself to a new domestic policy. We have no full employment policy. We have no welfare reform policy. We have no national health policy. We have no urban revitalization policy. We have no aggressive affirmative action policy. We have no national solutions to the grinding problems of poverty and discrimination.

To paraphrase Winston Churchill, "Never have so many expected so much and received so little."

A limited jobs program is not enough. An enlightened African policy is not enough. An expanded housing policy is not enough. A handful of top black appointments is not enough. An open style without substantive change is not enough. And it is not enough to do better than Nixon or Ford. Black people didn't vote for Nixon and didn't vote for Ford. They voted for President Carter, and it is not enough for President Carter to be just a little better than his predecessors.

Black people, having tasted the sweetness of victory in November, resent the sour taste of disappointment in July. Black people and poor people resent the stress on balanced budgets instead of balanced lives. We resent unfulfilled promises of jobs, compromises to win conservative support, and the continued acceptance of high unemployment.

Our resentment is fueled by impatience. We who have been patient for so long are finally running out of patience. The cries of pain from impoverished rural areas and urban slums ring out, and cannot be stilled by minor measures. Our longing for true equality will not cease, nor will it be diverted by stylistic flourishes.

In some ways, ours has been a learning experience. Black people are learning the callousness of political reality. We are learning that electing a president is not enough. We are learning that the forces of entrenched power will not easily accommodate our demands for change. We are learning that we must raise our voices and must use our political power with the same determination as do those who oppose us. We are learning that even an administration sympathetic to our needs and in harmony with our aspirations needs sustained pressure.

We are here in Washington to apply some of that pressure. We are here in Washington to call on this administration to fulfill its promises. We are here in Washington to recall this administration to what we feel is its true spirit, the spirit of social reform and racial equality. We are here in Washington to help it escape from the evils of premature political compromise, narrow fiscal conservatism, and indefinite delays in implementing reforms. We are here to file our claim, to collect on the campaign promises made in black churches and black neighborhoods.

We understand that the nature of the political process is such that all of our needs cannot be met at once. But we call on the administration to start sending signals that indicate it understands our needs and will make them its own.

One such signal should be the immediate withdrawal of the disastrous proposal to abolish the Electoral College in favor of direct popular election of the president. This seemingly democratic change would have undemocratic results. It would weaken the political power of the cities and the poor, and it would unbalance our political system. Do away with the Electoral College, and in 1980 the black vote will not make the difference it did in 1976.

It is unseemly for an administration that owes its existence to solid black electoral support to propose a new system whose effect would be to sabotage that support by diluting black voting power. And it is outrageous that the Congress has forced the administration to compromise its plan for a system of universal election day registration.

Another signal should be for the administration to come up with a serious program to save our nation's cities. The so-called urban crisis has become almost a cliché, stripped of meaning by repetition and misunderstanding.

There are those who believe the urban crisis is really just a fiscal crisis, and that shoveling federal dollars into city treasuries will solve it. But the problem goes far deeper, for the urban crisis has a human face to it. It is a crisis of national morality and of our national willingness to tolerate poverty and despair. And it is the direct result of over two decades of conscious public and private policies designed to depopulate cities and strip them of their economic capabilities.

Public and private policies moved population and job opportunities to the suburbs, and at the same time restocked the cities with poor people. Now there is general recognition that the process has gone too far. An energy-dependent society is beginning to realize that energy-efficient cities are necessary once more. The suburban dream has become tarnished, and middle-class people are again looking to the cities, where abandoned housing and cheap land are economically tempting to developers.

Race and economics once more interact to the detriment of
the black poor. Black slums have suddenly become targets for "re-
habilitation." Speculators reap profits while black homeowners
and renters are squeezed by the cycle of high demand, rising land
values, and higher property taxes.

If our cities are dying, it is not through natural death or even
self-inflicted suicide; it is through local policies aimed at killing
inner-city neighborhoods that they may be reborn for the benefit
of the well-off. HUD's [Department of Housing and Urban De-
velopment] tougher policy ensuring that block grants are used, as
the law demands, for poor people's housing is a commendable attempt to counter this growing phenomenon.

The process of saving the cities must not be a process of driving
out the poor to house the middle class, but a process of helping the
poor to become middle income. The ultimate future of our cities
and of our nation may depend upon the success of that effort.

We stepped to the edge of the abyss the other day, when the
plug was pulled on New York's electricity. The looting that occurred could have happened in any city in our country. All our
cities contain large numbers of people who have no stake in this
society, who are without jobs or hope, whose despair and anger
simmer continually, until it boils over, past the limits of accepted
behavior.

They are the victims of a society that willfully destroys its own
cities. The destruction they wrought was a more violent mirror
image of the destruction of lives and neighborhoods caused by
impersonal forces in our society—discrimination, unemployment, poverty. Lawlessness cannot be condoned, but our society

must draw the right conclusion from such terrible incidents: People have to be assured of a stake in the society; they must have jobs and decent housing if we want them to act in conformity with society's rules. The resources that will be spent to repair the damages could have been better spent in preventive programs that might have avoided the disaster.

But the tragedy in New York offers the president an opportunity to exercise bold leadership. We ask tonight that President Carter signal to the nation his concern for the cities and for the poor who live in them by going to New York; by speaking with the looters and the looted in the South Bronx, Harlem, and Bedford-Stuyvesant. A nation of cities is adrift in confusion and the president of all the people has to show his concern. He has to show he understands the despair and the anger, the hopes and the needs, of the urban poor. Yes, if the president can go to Clinton and to Yazoo City, he can go to New York.

We call on the president and the Congress to formulate a national urban policy that deals with the human problems of people who live in cities. Cities have to be saved, not for those who abandoned them and then changed their minds, but for those who live in them today.

And a national urban policy cannot be restricted to brick-and-mortar showpieces, or to further wasteful revenue-sharing programs. It must have three major components:

1. Federally supported and directed increases in basic social services—health, education, transportation, and youth programs,

2. Massive creation of housing opportunities for low-
   and moderate-income families, within a national housing policy that assures a decent, safe, and sanitary
   home for every family, and

3. A federal urban economic-development program that
   includes guaranteed jobs for all who can work, and
   an income-assistance system.

Finally, the administration should signal the nation's poor that
their interests will be met by meaningful reform of the welfare
system that is supposed to provide assistance to those most in
need, but does not. Candidate Carter called it a "disgrace," and
President Carter has ordered his administration to come up with
a reform proposal.

The basic outlines of the administration's package have been
made public, and they indicate that a real change is not in sight.

Although the reform was to result in a system that would be
equitable, simple to administer, promote family stability, and help
the poor, we are likely to have to fight a plan that is inequitable,
an administrative nightmare, promotes family instability, and
leaves many poor people worse off.

This plan founders on major conceptual flaws. Among them
are the mandates to keep a ceiling on costs no greater than present welfare-related programs, categorization of the poor, and a
work requirement. Such measures would continue to stigmatize
poor people while perpetuating negative myths about the poor.
And a bad plan may be made even worse. There was one proposal

to eliminate the federal housing subsidy program in order to transfer the money to the welfare program, a step that makes no sense at all. It would have destroyed already underfunded federal housing programs while further distorting welfare reform; and like other elements of the welfare reform plan, it would take from some poor people to give to other poor people.

The core of the welfare reform proposal links work to welfare, and thus perpetuates the vicious myth that poor people don't want to work. The fact is that poor people do want to work and do work. The fact is that poor people are as work-oriented as middle-class people.

Our purpose tonight is not to further criticize a bad plan but to offer an alternative that would benefit poor people and the nation.

The National Urban League is on record in support of a long-range plan to use a refundable-credit income tax as the means of assuring a minimum income level beneath which no family could fall. We continue to support that plan, but recognizing that political reality now prevents its acceptance, we call tonight for an interim plan that would supplement the present welfare system and ease the plight of poor people while putting in place structures for ultimate reform.

Our interim plan includes four major steps:

1. A massive job-creation program. We should have an expanded federal program of public service jobs, and job-creation incentives to private industry, targeted to high unemployment areas.

2. Food stamp expansion. The food stamp program has become a major source of income assistance. By eliminating the cash requirement, simplifying and broadening eligibility, and launching an aggressive outreach program, food stamps can become the vehicle for helping all of the poor and near-poor.

3. Major improvements in social insurance programs, including a national health insurance plan. Extending and improving programs that cushion the effects of unemployment and economic losses due to health problems will reduce the numbers of people forced to resort to welfare assistance.

4. A refundable tax credit. Ultimately, we envisage this as a means to drastically shrink the welfare rolls, but a start can be made now by using the tax system to provide modified income assistance.

Thus, by institutionalizing a refundable tax credit and applying it to grants for low-income families, even a modest grant would remove significant numbers of people from the welfare rolls while providing aid for those whose welfare benefits are inadequate and those who are poor or near-poor and do not receive welfare payments. This proposal would shrink the welfare rolls and would reduce the dependence on the welfare system through a more equitable tax system.

This interim plan would be real reform. By instituting this plan, the administration can refuse to become part of the institutional retreat from civil rights that is infecting the nation. In almost all sectors of national life we see former friends relaxing into indifference, and former foes back on the attack. National policies of neglect and recession have combined to make many people in the private sector less concerned with fulfilling their responsibilities.

The Congress seems more anxious to ban busing, to limit affirmative action programs, and to bar Medicaid funds for abortions than it is to improve the schools, enforce civil rights, or to enable meaningful life after birth. But, that same Congress was giving every indication of being willing to pour billions of dollars down the drain on the B–1 bomber before the president's bold and farsighted decision not to go ahead with production.

The symbol of institutional retreat is the Supreme Court. Once the proud defender of the rights of minorities and the disadvantaged, this Nixon-dominated court has become a source of denial of equal opportunities. The protector of our rights has slowly slid into the position of becoming the enemy of those rights.

The Court has retreated to the cramped narrow legalisms of supposed neutrality and objectivity. It has formulated the legal doctrine of "intent to discriminate" as a replacement for the more realistic legal requirement of proving discriminatory effects. In its last term, the Court upheld discriminatory zoning laws and discriminatory seniority systems. It denied to poor women the opportunity for abortion available to more affluent women, and it is shocking for the administration and the Congress to have supported the Court in this callous act.

It is in this Court then, so vastly different from the Warren Court that protected and extended civil rights, that the Bakke case [*Regents of the University of California v. Bakke*] will be decided.

We urge the administration to recognize the importance of this case and the issues involved by filing an amicus brief asking the Court to uphold the university's admissions program.

By the standards of legality, morality, and plain common sense, affirmative action programs are legitimate and necessary. And the intensity of the opposition to affirmative action is yet another example of the painful fact that the national mood still resists accommodation to the just needs of black and minority people. It still resists making necessary changes in our society to provide equal opportunity. The national search for roots is degenerating into mere nostalgia, instead of drawing lessons from the hardships forced upon our forebears and those of other ethnic groups.

And yet, because we hear the true call of our roots, because we draw inspiration from those who came before us and on whose accomplishments we build, we are unshakable in our determination to overcome. While we continue to impress upon the administration, the Congress, and the public and private sectors the justice of our cause, we have another job to do.

We must capitalize on the latent strengths of the black community. We must marshal our considerable economic and political power to improve our communities. We must bend every effort to instill in our young people devotion to excellence and a determination to succeed.

Those of us in leadership positions have a still larger responsibility. We cannot lessen our pressures for constructive change.

We cannot allow our personal or political loyalties to deflect us from the task of fighting for our rights. This applies as much to local leadership as it does to the national leadership of black institutions.

It is in this context that we must urge our black brothers and sisters in government to recognize the important role they can play. We are proud of them. Every announcement from the White House of the appointment of a black person to a federal position was met with pride. At long last there are enough black people at the higher echelons of government to form a critical mass capable of exerting a major influence on policy; most of these black federal executives come from backgrounds of militant activism, and the fervor and passion they brought to the civil rights movement must continue to characterize their actions.

Just as they were on guard for civil rights twenty-four hours a day, so, too, must they continue that vigilance in their new jobs. Just as they once prodded the executive branch, the Congress, and the courts with ceaseless demands for change, so, too, must they continue to raise the kinds of issues we have raised tonight.

Black federal executives are uniquely situated to become catalysts of change. They can maximize their strengths by coming together in an informal network of conscious interdependence and shared resources. All of our nation's institutions have run on the wheels of a well-oiled "buddy system" of mutual protection and mutual aid that excluded blacks and other minorities. So the inevitable lesson is that black and minority officials should come together in a similar system of shared support that will increase the influence of black executives and, more importantly, of the policies they are fighting for.

I cannot urge greater mutuality and cooperation among black federal executives without recognizing the need for closer cooperation among national black leadership. With a national mood that ranges from indifference to hostility, with crucial national decisions being made without due consideration of their impact on black people and with black institutional strength diluted because of lack of unified strategies, it is time for black leadership to come together once again.

On those occasions when we have coordinated strategies, such as last year's voter-registration campaign, we have been successful. It is time now to extend that success to other areas and other issues. It is time now for national black civil rights leadership to come together in a revived leadership group, in structured, planned meetings of heads of national organizations to pool our strengths and strategies.

So I call tonight on my colleagues to join with me in a meeting next month to begin the process of coordination on behalf of all of America's black and poor people. Our meetings should be held in private. They should deal with issues and strategies. They should be structured around the concerns of our constituents.

I am confident they will share my belief that it is imperative for black leadership to create a new structure that will enable us to act in unison and to maximize our efforts on behalf of our constituents. For if we don't do it, who will? We can call on the president to push for social changes, we can call on the Congress, we can call on the private sector; but in the last analysis what must be done, we must do ourselves. We need alliances and coalitions, but the initiative and the urgency must be ours.

We take our cue from Frederick Douglass,* who wisely counseled:

> Who would be free, themselves must strike the blow. . . . You know that liberty given is never so precious as liberty sought for and fought for. The man outraged is the man to make the outcry. Depend on it, men will not care much for a people who do not care for themselves.

I am confident that we can succeed, we shall overcome. The path, as always, will be difficult, but it is an American path, and that is why I am confident.

Last year I was in South Africa and two weeks ago I was in Russia. Seeing oppressive dictatorships of the right and the left convinces me that however far America may be from attaining its national goals and ideals, America is fertile soil for human fulfillment.

The plane that brought me home from Russia landed in New York during the blackout. The lights were out all over the city. But despite the inconvenience and the attendant problems, I'd rather

---

* Frederick Douglass was the great nineteenth-century black American abolitionist and statesman.

be here in the United States with the lights out than behind the Iron Curtain with the lights on. We have many just criticisms to make of our nation, but this speech could not be given in Russia or South Africa, and we could not dissent from national policies or pressure national leadership in Russia or South Africa.

Having visited such countries that are built on vicious denial of human rights, I take heart from our new national policy of worldwide support for the sanctity of human rights. When a Vorster kills young black people in Soweto, when a Brezhnev sends dissenters to prison camps, when an Amin senselessly slaughters his own people, all mankind is diminished. All mankind bleeds on the rack of the torturers, whoever they may be and wherever they may commit their crimes.

But this new American crusade for human rights and decency in the world must not become prey to hypocrisy and to cynicism. Our nation cannot call for respect for human rights while it lacks the moral courage to save its own cities, its own poor, its own minorities whose rights are trampled upon. The real moral equivalent of war in our times is the moral challenge to construct a just and equal society.

So our concern with human rights in the world must be joined by similar concern for basic human rights here at home. As long as our society denies equality of opportunity for its minorities, jobs for all who can work, and income security for all who need it, our advocacy of human rights will be met by scorn throughout the world. We cannot preach at others and sin ourselves.

It is the mission of the Urban League movement to remind our nation of this, and to toil on behalf of black people, of minorities, of all poor people. As we begin this conference, let us be mindful of that mission. Let us not forget who we are, from whence we came, and why we are here.

Most of us at this conference are working; our incomes place us in the middle class. We are educated; we are among DuBois's* talented tenth, and among us are found many of the black intelligentsia. We are professionals, semiprofessionals, blue- and white-collar workers; we represent business, labor, public and private sectors.

Our forebears were slaves. Our parents struggled to put us where we are. We are the first or second generation of our families to earn degrees. We are just a step ahead of the fathers and mothers, brothers and sisters who helped us. We know our roots. We know the years of toil and sweat; we know the ghettos from which we came; we remember the inferior segregated schools, the inequitable welfare system, the walls of discrimination in jobs and housing. Yes, we know all of this firsthand and because we know what it means to be black and poor in this society, we are painfully aware that our personal gains are tenuous and insecure. We know we cannot breathe easy while our brothers and sisters are still under the heel of poverty and hardship and discrimination.

We are here at this conference then, not for ourselves, but for them. We are here on behalf of our brothers and sisters, some of whom don't know who we are or what we're about, but they send

---

* W. E. B. DuBois was the great intellectual and activist whose ideas and words profoundly influenced blacks' twentieth-century freedom struggle.

us a message, an urgent message, to lead, to produce, to make
their futures brighter and more secure. They're depending on us.
Who will speak for them? Who will fight for them? In a society
that consigns black people to the bottom rung, it is the Urban
League and other institutions in the black community that stand
by their goals, their interests, their needs.

So we're here in Washington to work for the brothers and the
sisters. We're not here to party or to play, but to plan and to pressure. We have to demonstrate that we have not forgotten our
blackness, our roots, the poverty of our people. We are a movement with a mission, and as we begin this conference, let us recall
James Weldon Johnson's* invocation of remembrance of homage
to roots sunk deep and true:

> *God of our weary years,*
>
> *God of our silent tears,*
>
> *Thou who has brought us thus far on our way,*
>
> *Thou who has by Thy might*
>
> *Led us into the light,*
>
> *Keep us forever in the path, we pray.*

---

* James Weldon Johnson was a Renaissance figure whose careers included
professor, diplomat in the administration of President Theodore Roosevelt,
and secretary of the NAACP. He wrote the lines ending the speech—part of
the poem "Lift Ev'ry Voice and Sing," which became the Negro National
Anthem when his brother, John Rosamond Johnson, set the words to music.

DECLARING OUR
INTERDEPENDENCE

1979

"**N**ineteen hundred seventy-nine promises to be a year of crisis for America's black people."

So I stated in mid-January 1979 during a press conference called to discuss the National Urban League's annual publication devoted to examining blacks' status, *The State of Black America.*

I was specifically referring to the combination of congressional resistance to enacting legislation to reduce poverty, legal attacks on affirmative action, and the economic data that showed how little overall progress blacks had made during the latter half of the 1970s. The recession of the early to mid–1970s had exacted a severe toll on black America. On the one hand, the number of black families earning middle-class incomes had increased from 1.2 million to 1.5 million as more blacks moved into and up the ranks of the white-collar job ladder. But that good news was swamped by a broad tide of alarming developments that actually reduced the overall percentage of middle-class black families from 26 percent to 24 percent. While the median income of white families had increased by 2 percent from 1974 to early 1979, that of black families had not increased at all. Meanwhile, black unemployment, especially among males, had risen sharply. As I spoke that January, the unemployment rate for black adults was 9.2 percent, well above the national rate of 5.8 percent; and officially, nearly 33 percent of black teens were jobless. Equally worrisome was the crowding over the decade of the black poor into the urban ghettos, which themselves were becoming more and more isolated from easy access to where the jobs were. By the end of the 1970s, U.S. Census data indicated that nearly 56 percent of the nation's 25 million blacks lived in metropolitan areas—and that more than half of them lived in those areas' poorest and most dilapidated neighborhoods.

Yet the severe domestic crises blacks faced were to be unexpectedly overshadowed that year by two bitter controversies involving blacks and the Carter administration's foreign policy.

Both had to do with the intractable Israeli-Palestinian conflict. The first was the resignation in August of Andrew Young as ambassador to the United Nations. As one of Martin Luther King, Jr.'s closest lieutenants, a former congressman, and a former mayor of Atlanta, Young had a large following among blacks and white liberals and moderates. In addition, he was a close personal friend of President Carter: His endorsement of Carter's candidacy in early 1976 had substantially boosted the political fortunes of the then little-known former Georgia governor. But in July 1979, Young had violated a cardinal rule of American diplomacy: He secretly met with the representative to the UN of the Palestine Liberation Organization (PLO) to discuss ways of breaking the Middle East stalemate. The U.S. government had long labeled the PLO a terrorist organization and had barred American diplomats from discussing any substantive issues with PLO representatives. The disclosure of Young's action quickly provoked widespread criticism from white individuals and organizations across the political spectrum, including leading American Jewish groups. That criticism, in turn, prompted statements of support for Young from a broad range of black elected officials, civil rights leaders, and other prominent figures—some of whom believed Young had acted with the tacit support of the Carter administration. Some blacks also criticized Jewish groups for trying to "dictate" what opinions blacks were to express on the Middle East. Kenneth B. Clarke, the eminent psychologist, went so far as to proclaim blacks' support of Young a "declaration of independence" from Jewish organizations' influence.

The Young resignation and ensuing controversy brought to the surface differences between blacks and Jews over several issues—particularly affirmative action, which blacks overwhelmingly supported and several leading Jewish organizations and individuals opposed—that had simmered throughout the 1970s. From the moment Young resigned, some Jewish and black leaders, including myself and Benjamin F. Hooks, the NAACP's executive director, sought to prevent the dispute from escalating into a complete rupture.

In September, those efforts suffered a sharp setback when both the Reverend Joseph E. Lowery, president of the Southern Christian Leadership Conference, and the Reverend Jesse L. Jackson, head of People United to Save Humanity (PUSH), separately traveled to the Middle East and met with several Arab leaders, including Yasir Arafat, the head of the PLO. During their meeting, Lowery and his SCLC delegation invited Arafat to attend conferences they said they were arranging in the United States, and at the end of their meeting led in the singing of the civil rights anthem, "We Shall Overcome." Jackson met with Arafat and told reporters covering the trip that he hoped to mediate a discussion of the conflict involving the PLO, the Carter administration, and Israeli government officials.

I decided then that I had to speak out forcefully against such misguided behavior; and the invitation to address the National Conference of Catholic Charities, which resulted in this speech, provided the perfect forum. First, I felt a responsibility to condemn ill-considered rhetorical support for terrorist groups that had murdered innocent civilians because such behavior was anathema to the nonviolent moral principles of the civil rights movement. Second, I also wanted to point out that these flirtations diverted resources and attention from an economic crisis that was ravaging blacks, especially the "vital survival issues" immediately affecting the black poor. I was eager to assert that rather than declarations of independence, what black Americans and America as a whole needed was "a declaration of interdependence" that would refocus our energies on reducing the accumulating social problems of America. Such a recognition of our common humanity and our mutual need was the only antidote to the ideology and practice of indifference that had already significantly undermined the promise of the civil rights revolution of the 1960s. My speech angered some black leaders, and they said so publicly. I welcomed the debate. That was perfectly in keeping with the long-standing tradition within black leadership of never hesitating to express disagreements over substantive issues. Those disagreements never endangered personal friendships. The willingness to publicly debate contentious issues allowed black Americans to consider the full dimensions of the issue. This speech was my contribution.

ANNUAL MEETING OF THE NATIONAL
CONFERENCE OF CATHOLIC CHARITIES
Kansas City, Missouri
October 15, 1979

L ike many of you, I was held spellbound last week watching the journey of His Holiness, Pope John Paul II, in our nation.

And, like many of you, I could not help but think back to 1960, when bigotry was an issue in the presidential campaign. If Jack Kennedy is elected president, some people said, the pope will be in the White House.

Well, Jack Kennedy was elected president of the United States, and the pope did come to the White House. But when he came in 1979 he was greeted warmly by a Southern Baptist president, Jimmy Carter.

The intervening years have seen a welcome decline in religious intolerance. Religion is no longer a factor in our national politics. Catholicism is no longer a handicap in politics, or in other aspects of our national life.

America has changed. But not enough. For if religious discrimination has faded, racial discrimination remains strong. It, too, has declined. But its grip retains a strong hold on many Americans. While it is no longer fashionable in many circles to admit to racism, we have to recognize that racism has been channeled to more subtle avenues. The result is continued disadvantage for blacks, Hispanics, and other minorities.

I am hopeful that the pope's visit will have some positive effect on the insidious racism that still finds a home in the minds of many Americans.

The pope took every opportunity to deliver an age-old message: Love thy neighbor, help the poor, feed the hungry. He called for a just society. He drew attention to the injustice in our society by going to the black ghetto in Harlem and the Puerto Rican barrio in the South Bronx. He went to the poorest and the humblest in our society—the victims of poverty and discrimination.

How will America react to that message of human liberty, equality, and dignity?

Will those who applauded him so vigorously in his public appearances and who cheered his motorcades so loudly follow his challenge?

Will they examine their own thoughts and acts and root out the racism that is so offensive to the human spirit?

Will they make the link between abstract principles of justice and their own actions?

I am hopeful they will, but only time will tell. We shall see whether the wave of firebombings and cross burnings ends. We shall see whether irrational racial distinctions disappear. And we shall see whether the new negativism that is gripping the American spirit fades.

For the pope's message comes at a time when Americans appear to have abandoned the quest for social justice and retreated into an antisocial privatism.

In the 1960s there was a general consensus, shared by whites and blacks alike, that an activist government should achieve full employment, reverse the effects of discrimination, and revitalize the cities. Today that consensus has been shattered. In its place we see the formation of a new negativism in America that calls for a weak, passive government; indifference to the plight of the poor; abandonment of affirmative action; and letting the cities twist slowly, slowly in the wind.

Make no mistake about it. Race is central to the rising support of the new negativism. People are not merely saying "no" to high taxes and inflation, they are saying "no" to inclusion of black and brown people into the mainstream. And behind that "no" are the vestiges of a racism that blights American life and casts a long shadow over our pretensions to speak on behalf of human rights throughout the world.

Perhaps the most insidious idea fostered by the new negativism, and one that is shared by too many Americans, is the strange idea that blacks and browns have made so much progress that special efforts are no longer needed. This is something that demands further analysis, because it is so pervasive an attitude in our society.

Even friends of the civil rights movement have urged us to stop complaining so loudly. By stressing the extreme plight of the poorest among us, they say, we foster a negativist mood in the country. They claim politicians and the public will conclude that efforts to fight poverty fail. Therefore, the new programs we need will be rejected.

I cannot accept that strategy. I can't accept sweeping the misery of millions of black and brown Americans under the rug in the vain hopes that the new negativists will look more kindly on modest reform programs.

Stressing the positive would just result in what is happening anyway—the mistaken belief that our racial, economic, and urban problems are solved.

So let us look for a moment at the thesis that there has been significant black progress, progress that should be trumpeted loudly to a self-satisfied nation.

Let us look at the thesis that celebrates the gains of a few but ignores the continued sufferings of the many.

Let us start with jobs. Work is the measure of a person's worth in our society. It is the key that opens all other doors. How much progress have we made in employment?

Some of us have done well. Black men and women in both the public and the private sectors are holding job titles and receiving paychecks unheard of for black people a decade or so ago.

But they form a small part of the black workforce. The masses of black people are still in the worst jobs our society offers. Black workers are twice as likely as whites to be in low-pay, low-skill jobs, and less than half as likely as whites to be in the jobs that count in America.

The black unemployment rate is higher than it was when we marched on Washington for jobs and freedom. Black people are experiencing Depression-level unemployment. With the nation now entering a new recession, black people still have not recovered from the last one.

Black youth have become an endangered, lost generation. Unemployment rates for black young people approach 60 percent in our cities.

Income is a basic measure of progress. Some of us have made great strides. A few have reached parity with whites. We are often told about the 9 percent of black families in the upper-income brackets. But what about the other 91 percent? How are they doing?

A third are poor—three times the white rate. The majority are near-poor. They earn less than the government itself says is needed for a minimum adequate–living standard. Half a million black people were added to the ranks of the poor in the 1970s. And in this International Year of the Child the majority of black children are growing up in families experiencing severe economic hardship.

The shameful fact this nation must face is that the gap between whites and blacks is growing instead of closing. At the end of the sixties the typical black-family income was 61 percent of the typical white-family income. Today, it is down to 57 percent.

Education is another basic area. Twenty-five years after *Brown*, more black children attend racially isolated schools than in 1954.

In some cities, black high school dropouts outnumber graduates. Many school systems program black youth for failure. Many of our children spend twelve years in schools and classrooms indifferent to their fate and then cannot pass minimum reading and arithmetic requirements.

Yes, more blacks are attending college than ever before. But the majority are in two-year community colleges while the majority of whites are in four-year schools that put them on career ladders denied to blacks. Black enrollments in medical and professional schools are declining while total enrollments rise.

Has there been progress in housing? Some. More black families are living in decent housing, and some are living in suburbs that never saw a black face after the maid's quitting time. But the point is whether black progress is real when measured against standards enjoyed by white Americans.

By that standard, there is still an intolerable gap. One out of five black families live in housing that the government says is physically deficient. HUD says blacks are three times as likely as whites to live in housing that has serious deficiencies. And blacks are twice as likely as whites to pay more than they can afford to get decent housing.

It is clear that the glass of racial progress is only half full.

It is clear that blacks remain disadvantaged.

It is clear that race continues to be a major determining factor in our society.

It is clear that, for all the progress some of us have made, half of all black Americans are boat people without boats, cast adrift in a hostile ocean of discrimination, unemployment, and poverty.

So we can't be satisfied with talk of progress. Not when so many of us have not experienced that progress. Not when our goal is full equality, not just progress.

We've got to make the 1980s a decade in which black people finally enjoy full equality. We've got to organize behind an agenda for the 1980s. An agenda that includes a national full-employment policy; a massive drive for affirmative action in all aspects of national life; a national youth-development policy that gives hope and skills to young people denied both; a national health policy that assures high-quality health care for all; and a housing program that assures a decent living environment for all.

Those—and other major steps—must be at the core of our agenda for the 1980s.

And we've got to recognize that our agenda demands construction of powerful alliances. We can't do it alone. We shouldn't have to try to do it alone.

The black agenda for the 1980s transcends race, sex, and region. It is "black" only in the sense that blacks are disproportionately poor. Our agenda is directed at helping all of America's poor and deprived citizens—most of whom are white. It is an agenda that is in the national interest, an agenda that will make America a stronger, better nation.

To that end, black people must concentrate on forging alliances with other segments of our society for the good of all.

We must reach out to other groups who share our problems. An obvious ally is America's large Hispanic population, which also suffers discrimination and disproportionate poverty. But other groups share our agenda, too, and every effort must be made to cross the artificial barriers of race and ethnicity and organize around issues of common concern.

I am concerned that our traditional alliances are under pressure these days. At the core of the civil rights alliance of the fifties and sixties were blacks, the labor movement, and the Jewish community. Now the events following Andy Young's resignation have led to deep strains in that alliance.

While some have categorized statements on black-Jewish relations as being a declaration of independence, I believe we need a declaration of interdependence. For black or white, Christian or Jew, urban or rural, our destinies are linked and intertwined. We must strengthen the ties that bind us, not weaken them.

We should be very clear about the need to combat racism, anti-Semitism and religious bigotry in all its forms. The confusions of the past several weeks must not be allowed to polarize the civil rights alliance. Nor must they be allowed to heighten or to release feelings of racism, anti-Semitism, or religious bigotry.

The only ones who benefit from black-Jewish tensions are the enemies of both groups. It is time to stop providing joy to the cross burners and bomb throwers. It is time to strengthen the traditional, fruitful alliance between blacks and Jews.

That alliance must be based on mutual respect, concern for each group's vital interests, and a refusal to categorize all blacks or Jews for the actions or statements of some. We will disagree about some issues. There will always be occasional disagreements over issues among members of any alliance. But those disagreements must be in the nature of family disputes that do not affect the overall harmony of our relations.

Black-Jewish relations should not be endangered by ill-considered flirtations with terrorist groups devoted to the extermination of Israel. The black civil rights movement is based on nonviolent moral principles. It has nothing in common with groups whose claim to legitimacy is compromised by cold-blooded murder of innocent civilians and schoolchildren.

Black people have the right and the duty as citizens to help shape our foreign policy. No one has the right to limit our involvement to predetermined "black" issues. But as we frame our foreign policy options, we must be sensitive to the basic interests of our domestic allies and consistent with our historic values of justice and morality.

In the past several weeks we've seen more concern exhibited about Palestinian refugee camps than about America's ghettos.

We've seen more concern about the PLO's [Palestine Liberation Organization] goals than about black America's aspirations for equality. And we've seen more concern about Yasir Arafat's future than about the future of the millions of black kids growing up in poverty.

Given the recent preoccupation of some black leaders with these concerns, it becomes more important than ever that the black community and its allies focus strongly on the immediate problems facing the black poor.

Our agenda for the 1980s comprises the vital survival issues for black people, issues that can't be allowed to be displaced by sideshows. That agenda for the 1980s depends on the success with which we can cut across racial, class, and regional lines to unite Americans behind our blueprint for a progressive future. And it is essential that voluntary social welfare agencies join us in making our agenda a reality.

Those of us working in voluntary social welfare agencies know at first hand of the depths of misery in our urban wastelands. We know firsthand that America's poor face desperate conditions— victimized by poverty, by joblessness, by bad housing, inadequate health care and schooling, and a host of other ills. And we know that those conditions are the result not of individual faults but of *systems* that place increasing burdens on the shoulders of those least equipped to bear them.

To be silent, then, is to be accomplices in the crimes against the poor. It is the affirmative duty of social welfare agencies to speak out on behalf of their constituents, to educate the public to the needs they face, and to pressure public and private power to become more responsive to the needs of our society's forgotten poor.

This, to me, is the primary challenge facing the voluntary sector in the coming decade.

The issue is not service *or* advocacy. It is whether our social welfare establishment is compassionate enough, caring enough, and willing enough to embrace the overriding principle of services *and* advocacy.

I believe it is. I believe that the idealism and the sensitivity that lead professionals and volunteers into this form of public service are alive enough to embrace the duty to fight for the larger interests of America's dispossessed.

I believe that social welfare agencies will perceive that it is not enough to bandage the walking wounded, but to end the war on the poor, indeed, to wage a war on poverty, discrimination, and disadvantage.

Our society has produced material riches beyond the dreams of past ages. But it has also created reservoirs of misery and need that must offend the sensibilities of civilized people. It has left millions upon millions stranded in hopelessness and despair.

They cannot be denied. We in the voluntary sector can deny them only at our own peril. We hear from the crevices of our nation's poverty-stricken ghettos the poignant plea for services and advocacy. We hear from the dark corners people crying out asking, pleading: Is there no balm in Gilead? Is there no physician there?

Hear their plea, let your response ring loud and clear. Let your response be, "Yes, there is a balm in Gilead—there is a doctor to heal a sick society."

Respond to that plea for help with renewed commitment and dedication, with a spirit of understanding and with devotion to services and advocacy on behalf of those in need.

Speaking to the poor of the South Bronx, Pope John Paul II said: "I come here because I know of the difficult conditions of your existence, because I know that your lives are marked by pain."

Let us then work together to end the pain of the poor. Let us speak forcefully on their behalf. Let us challenge the negativism in our society with a burning, passionate, moral vision of a society that is truly an integrated, pluralistic, open society.

To that end, your duties and responsibilities are clear. You have a charge to keep, a calling to fulfill, a rendezvous with a just and righteous cause.

As you return to those tasks, be steadfast, strong, and of good cheer. May you neither stumble nor falter; rather will you mount up with wings as eagles; let us run and not be weary, and walk together children, and not faint.

CIVIL RIGHTS

Past Gains, Present Uncertainty

1981

As the 1980s opened, Ronald Reagan, expertly employing the rhetoric and images of a mythic American individualism, swept into the presidency. The former California governor fractured the traditional Democratic coalition and won every sector of the country, amassing a total of 489 electoral votes to just forty-nine for President Carter. His victory vindicated the twenty-year effort of the so-called Goldwater conservatives to wrest control of the Republican Party from its moderate, Eastern establishment wing and gave them the political platform they needed to pursue their ultimate goal: to destroy the structures and policies of New Deal liberalism that had guided American politics and American society for half a century.

More directly, Ronald Reagan's victory reflected the American electorate's anger at a series of humbling events and developments during the 1970s that seemed to mock America's power and certainly sapped the American people's morale and sense of their destiny. The government's moral authority had been sapped by the Watergate scandal and its military self-confidence by the chaotic retreat from Vietnam. The economy had suffered a decade of inflation, the oil shock of 1973, and two severe recessions. The most humiliating event of all was what came to be known as the Iran hostage crisis— the plundering in November 1979 of the American embassy in Teheran and the kidnapping of fifty-two American diplomats, service members, and private citizens by Islamic fundamentalists allied with Iran's theocratic regime. The hostages were held captive for 444 days—through the American presidential campaign and election. The Iranian regime released them almost exactly at the moment of Reagan's inauguration on January 20, 1981.

Another mighty contribution to the Reagan landslide was the rising hostility of many whites to completing the unfinished work of the civil rights revolution of the 1960s. The white conservative coalition of nonprofit legal foundations and think tanks that arose in reaction to the civil rights victories of the 1960s had fashioned a deft campaign in the courts of law and the court of public opinion to disparage affirmative action in higher education and in government contracting as "reverse discrimination." They contended that laws prohibiting discrimination were sufficient to erase the effects of an entire century's concentrated antiblack bigotry in both public and private sectors of American society. In this area of public policy, Reagan signaled he would reverse what had become accepted government standards. His August 1980 appearance at the state fair in Neshoba County, Mississippi—the county where the infamous 1964 murder of the three civil rights workers had occurred—to praise "states' rights" presaged the posture toward civil rights his administration would follow for the next eight years.

There is no doubt that Reagan's sunny personality and boundless public optimism soothed and inspired an electorate that, while not supportive of the entire conservative program, desperately wished to escape the failed national governments of the 1970s. His appeal captured the interest of some number of black Americans, too: He drew 12 percent of blacks' votes. Although this figure continued the downward trajectory of the GOP's attraction to black voters, it seemed to signal the willingness of some blacks to try Reagan as an alternative to the seeming malaise gripping the nation. It also helped that Reagan was vouched for by a small group of newly visible and assertive black conservatives who stood in opposition not only to the progressive views of the black civil rights and political leadership but to moderate Republicanism as well.

I knew firsthand that it was almost impossible to personally dislike Ronald Reagan. In August 1980, having readily accepted the Urban League's invitation to speak at its annual conference in New York, he spent forty-five minutes visiting with me at New York Hospital–Cornell Medical Center, where I was recovering from the attempt on my life; and he brought with him his secretary, Ida Gaston, who had been my friend and neighbor in the University Homes housing project in Atlanta.

The following year, after he was wounded by a would-be assassin, I was honored to repay this personal kindness. James Baker, his excellent chief of staff, arranged for me to be the first private citizen to visit him as he recuperated in the hospital in Washington. I also wrote a brief op-ed piece for the *Washington Post* of April 5, 1981. I said that as "one who has been the victim of a similar attack, I know what the president is going through, and he has my prayers and hopes for a full recovery." I went on to say:

> The president is president of all the people, and all of the people have a stake in his ability to discharge the functions of his office. We all have a stake in the stability of the government. We all realize that our freedoms are endangered when dangerous weapons in the hands of people with twisted minds replace the political process.

I wanted to express in the strongest terms my outrage at the vicious attack on him as an individual and on the office of the president, because I believed it was my duty not only as an individual but also as the leader of a black organization. Black Americans, who have endured horrific violence throughout their history in America, have always been the most fervent loyalists of its democratic political processes.

After his election in November, President Reagan had included me in the broad group of people he consulted for suggestions on which domestic issues to target in his inaugural address. And all through his White House years, my sharp policy disagreements with his administration did not preclude my being invited to state dinners, nor did they preclude James Baker from always being accessible to me on matters of importance to the Urban League.

Nonetheless, it had become apparent by the time the Urban League convened its annual conference in mid-July of 1981 in Washington that the president's personal appeal and my access to the administration weren't going to lead to substantive policies addressing black America's needs. This was especially true in two areas. One concerned the persistent unemployment ravaging poor black communities. Nationally, the unemployment rate had remained twice that of whites, and for black teens it hovered above 30 percent officially, but in many communities it reached 50 percent and higher. This structural poverty ensnaring the black poor didn't result from a "culture of poverty" among blacks. Its origin and persistence was far simpler: the transformation of the American economy, and particularly the decline of factory jobs that had once constituted the first step into the job market for the urban poor.

The other major concern of the keynote address was the president's concerted effort to go beyond merely avoiding support for needed legislation on civil rights and other domestic

initiatives, instead actively rolling back the legislative and policy gains blacks had made whenever and wherever he could.
Black America had not faced such a hostile administration,
and one whose regressive policies clearly had the support of a
substantial segment of the electorate, since that of Woodrow
Wilson seventy years before. That made it the more imperative
to rebut the falsehoods of the Reagan policies and put forward
cogent reasons for returning to the progressive-policy track.

This speech was important to me because it would mark
the end of my service as president of the National Urban
League. A month later, I would announce that I was resign-
ing from the organization and the search for my successor
would begin. At the time, only three people knew of my
plans: my late wife, Shirley; Coy Eklund, chairman of the Urban League Board of Trustees and chairman and chief executive of the Equitable Life Assurance Society; and Lisle C.
Carter, the trustees' vice chairman and president of the University of the District of Columbia. Many people have as-
sumed I left the league because of the attempt on my life. But
had the shooting that occurred in Fort Wayne, Indiana, on
May 29, 1980, been a factor in my decision, I would never
have returned to the organization after my recovery. In fact,
my motivation for leaving was much more positive. I had
been in office for ten years and that was long enough. It was
time for me to pass the baton to new leadership and go on to
a new challenge: a partnership at Akin, Gump, Strauss,
Hauer & Feld, the Washington, D.C.–based law firm of my
longtime, treasured friend Robert S. Strauss. I could leave

without regret because I felt the league's national headquarters was more confident than when I got there, and its 100-plus affiliates across the country at its heart were strong and had effective leadership. The National Urban League was in good hands. My feeling was like that expressed in Timothy (2 Timothy 4:7): "I have fought a good fight, I have finished my course, I have kept the faith."

National Urban League Annual Conference
Washington, D.C.
July 19, 1981

*M*r. Chairman Coy Eklund, Mr. Conference Chairman Lisle Carter, Mr. Mayor Barry, Mr. Chairman of the City Council Arrington Dixon, Mr. Local Conference Chairman Jones, our local Board Chairman Dr. Howard Davis, our local Washington UL President Jerry Page, dais guests—Urban Leaguers all:

Last year's NUL Conference was the first in my decade in the Urban League that I did not attend personally. I saw the proceedings on videotape. I spoke to the conference on audiotape, but all the while I felt deeply deprived, for there can be no more vital experience than being among the people I love in this meeting of the movement I love.

But last year's experience also renewed my appreciation of the strength of the Urban League. Few organizations could sail through a crisis such as we faced last spring and summer. Few could demonstrate the depth of skills and experience that we did.

Our chairman, Coy Eklund, merits our deep appreciation for the way he helped our agency pull through. And we thank you very much. Coy, our dedicated trustees, and our 25,000 volunteers all provided encouragement and support far beyond the call of duty.

With their help, national and affiliate staff performed with the devotion to excellence and to results that typifies the Urban League. And John Jacob displayed a unique blend of grace under pressure, hard work, wisdom, and leadership that won the admiration of everyone—in and out of our movement. He deserves a special thanks from all of us for his superb job.

Thanks to your great efforts, the Urban League emerged from its crisis stronger than ever. So it is good to be here tonight, to salute you—not on tape, but in full, living color.

My first Urban League Conference address was in 1971. Then, too, it dealt with a conservative administration in Washington. But that administration, while hostile to black people, was pragmatic. It had to be. There was still a strong national consensus that operated to preserve black gains. The Congress was a bulwark against attempts to dismantle important social programs. We had a two-party system then.

Today, there is another conservative administration in Washington. But this time, much has changed.

This administration is wedded to an ideology of radical conservatism. This administration has introduced a new political vocabulary—"budget reconciliation," "truly needy," "supply-side economics," and other phrases. But it has dropped from the political vocabulary the one word that makes government relevant to the governed, the one word that grants legitimacy to its laws: "compassion."

This is not mere semantics. The administration's refusal to temper ideology with compassion makes it a clear and present danger to black people and to poor people.

Those are harsh words, but true ones. And they apply despite the obvious charm of the president. We must make a clear distinction between our political and ideological differences with President Reagan and our high personal regard for him. The president is a good man, a courageous man, and on a personal level, a compassionate man.

Not since Franklin Delano Roosevelt has America been led by so gifted a communicator. Not since Lyndon Baines Johnson has it been led by so skillful a politician. And not since Herbert Hoover has it been led by a president willing to sacrifice millions of people on the altar of an outmoded ideology.

Yes, outmoded. The president claims to be bringing us new ideas and new policies. But they are actually a recycled version of ideas and policies that were buried in the Great Depression. And with good reason.

What are the new ideas the administration is ramming down the throats of the nation? Get government off our backs. Give power and programs to the states. Federal programs have failed. Rely on the free enterprise system. Build more missiles.

Those are not ideas, they are slogans. Like most slogans, they contain a grain of truth. And like most slogans, they oversimplify and distort. They reinforce the meanest instincts of selfishness. They cut society loose from its moral bearings.

I say to you tonight, black people don't need to be told that government is on our backs because we know it has been by our side, helping to counterbalance the vicious racism that deprived us of our lives, our liberty, and our rights.

I say to you tonight, black people don't need to be told that power and programs should go to the states, because we know the few, feeble programs that have helped us were those mandated by Washington. It was the state and local governments that excluded us from everything from voting to paved streets. And it is they who will trample on our interests again if this administration dumps the programs we need into block grants.

I say to you tonight, black people don't need to be told federal programs have failed, because we know many have succeeded. The Pentagon may not be able to land helicopters in Iran, but the Food Stamp Program has fed the hungry; Social Security has wiped out poverty for most older citizens; CETA [Comprehensive Employment and Training Act] has put the jobless to work, compensatory education programs have improved reading scores of disadvantaged youth, and legal services has given poor people access to the justice system.

Black people don't need to be told to rely on the free enterprise system. We believe in the free enterprise system, we want to be part of it. We want our fair share of it.

And we know that will not happen without a federal government that pushes the private sector into affirmative action programs. It will not happen without a federal government that has set-asides for minority enterprises and job and training programs for the disadvantaged.

Black people don't need to be lectured about the need for economic growth. When others were talking of "an era of limits," "less is more," and "small is beautiful," we were saying "bake a bigger pie." We want economic growth. We know that in this America we will not get our fair share unless there is more for everyone. But we also know that we will not get our fair share just because there is more. America has managed to push us from the table of prosperity in good times as in bad.

So it is not enough just to have growth. What we want to know is "economic growth for whom?" JFK's quote, "A rising tide lifts all boats" is no answer. A rising tide lifts only those boats in the water; our boats are in the dry dock of America's economy. And we know we will be stranded on dry land, far from that rising tide, unless government steps in with the programs and protection that help launch us into the mainstream.

That will not happen with an economic program that gives to the wealthy in the vague hopes that some of it will trickle down to the poor. What little trickles down had dried up long before it reaches us.

Let us cut through the rhetoric of a supply-side economics that supplies misery to the poor: This administration's economic program amounts to a massive transfer of resources from the poor to the rich.

It takes money, programs, and opportunities from poor people and promises them in return an end to inflation and prosperity for all. It says to poor people: Give up the little you have today and we promise you a lot more in the by-and-by. Well, black people aren't buying pie-in-the-sky economics.

Last year Candidate Reagan came to the Urban League's annual conference. He cataloged the many economic problems our nation faces. And he said: "Let us make a compact among ourselves—a compact not to fight these problems on the backs of the poor."

But that is exactly what this jelly-bean budget does!

Candidate Reagan said: "Think of how discouraging it must be for those who have always had less. To now be told that they must further reduce their standard of living."

But that is exactly what this jelly-bean budget does!

Last month President Reagan said: "I do not intend to let America drift further toward economic segregation."

But that is exactly what this jelly-bean budget does!

When we look at this jelly-bean budget, we say to the president, in the words of the Psalmist: "Thou hast showed thy people hard things: Thou hast made us to drink the wine of astonishment."

A brief look at what happened to some of the major domestic programs will demonstrate that black people are the major victims of a budget that tears huge gaping holes in our safety net:

+ Social Security. The minimum benefit—a measly
$122 a month—is eliminated. Who gets hurt? Poor
black people who spent their working lives on their
knees cleaning floors. Disability benefits are tightened.
Who gets hurt? Workers who are injured or fall sick
and can't work anymore—a disproportionate number of them black.

+ Food stamps. A million people will lose their food stamps, millions more will have their benefits reduced. Who gets hurt? The working poor. Over a third of all food stamp recipients are black.

+ Public service jobs ended; CETA training cut back. Who gets hurt? Over a third of all CETA workers are black.

+ Medicaid is capped. Poor people will suffer reductions in access to health care. Who gets hurt? Over a third of Medicaid recipients are black.

+ Legal services. The administration wanted to kill it. But our compassionate Congress just cut its budget by two-thirds. Who gets hurt? People who can't afford a lawyer. Poor people. A third are black.

+ Welfare is cut and a forced work program authorized in the hope that unpleasant make-work jobs will drive people off the rolls. Who gets hurt? Almost half the recipients are black children and black mothers. Who gets hurt most? Working mothers who get small welfare checks to supplement their low earnings.

+ Education aid cut heavily. Who gets hurt? Disadvantaged children, over a third of them black.

Defenders of that budget will tell us black people are not being singled out. That's true. It's only poor people who are being victimized. And we are 12 percent of the population but a third of the poor—so we are the main victims.

We are told the nation can no longer afford to help the poor. But it can afford to throw 1.5 trillion dollars at the Pentagon over the next five years.

We are told social programs don't help poor people: They help the people in social service professions. Tell that to the families deprived of their food stamps, their welfare checks, their public service jobs.

We are told social programs breed dependency. Tell that to the working mothers who will have to quit their jobs or lose benefits. Tell it to young people in training programs who will lose their . chance to learn and to earn their way out of poverty. Tell it to sick people whose public health clinics are shut down.

We are told that it's bad to look to government for special help—everyone should be treated the same. Tell that to the affluent who will get huge tax cuts on top of their loopholes. Tell it to the corporations on welfare. Tell it to the special interests who still get their subsidies while poor people lose their lifelines.

Last month the Congress rushed this jelly-bean budget through. With no real debate, the programs that help the poor were cut to ribbons. With no real debate, years of slow, patient progress were swept out to sea by the rising tide of radical conservatism.

Never have so few taken so much from so many in so little time!

Where was the outcry against those outrages? Where were the Democrats? Where were the liberals? Where were the congressmen who once fought for the programs that give poor people opportunities?

With some honorable exceptions, they were engaged in a last-ditch fight to cut the president's three-year tax cut back to two years. They were in a last-ditch fight to save benefits for the middle class and farm interests. Roosevelt led a party concerned with the "ill-housed, ill-clad, ill-nourished." Today his successors are concerned with the upper middle class.

Democrats and Republicans alike need some arithmetic lessons. They need to learn that poll results still show significant public support for social programs that work.

They need to learn that when they cut social programs whose beneficiaries are one-third to one-half black, the remainder are white. Whites make up half to two-thirds of the victims of the cuts.

And if they don't care about blacks and poor whites, they should realize that this is just the beginning. Tax cuts combined with massive increases in defense spending mean more budget cuts down the road. And when the poor have no more programs left to cut, the cuts will start reaching into the middle class constituency the Democrats are now courting.

One last word for the Democrats who take the black vote for granted: An opposition that does not oppose is not worthy of governing.

But the silence extends well beyond a passive Congress. When aid to the arts is cut, there are full-page newspaper ads of protest. There are petitions, and loud protest. When an aggressive foreign policy is implemented, there is the same. But where are the voices raised on behalf of poor people? Where are the churches, the universities, the other sectors of our society that once marched with us and supported us?

And where is the enlightened business community? Will they keep their silence as the price for their tax cuts? Will they choose short-term profits over the long-term social stability that ultimately is the surest guarantee of the free enterprise system? Will they silently pocket billions in tax cuts without speaking out on behalf of poor working people who lose their food stamps?

The silence is frightening because the real issue extends beyond the specific budget cuts. The real issue is the grand design of substituting charity for entitlements, local tyranny for federal protection, and unbridled, law-of-the-jungle capitalism for a balanced cooperation between the public and private sectors.

Thus, the real issue is the nature of our society.

We of the National Urban League movement believe there is no contradiction between equality and liberty; between economic growth and social justice; between a strong defense and healthy cities; between government assistance and individual opportunities. We believe that a moral society requires compassion for the poor, economic justice, and racial equality.

We will play our part in the national dialogue about the future of the nation we love so much and for which we have sacrificed so much. We will do our part by following the biblical mandate to "open thy mouth, judge righteously, and plead the cause of the poor and needy."

But a dialogue means listening to opposing views as well, we will listen. Tomorrow the vice president will speak to us. Other high administration officials will also present their case. We welcome them.

We want to hear them address issues of concern to black people and to all Americans. We want to hear them explain their program. We want to hear them give us their vision of America and of black people's role in its future.

I hope they go beyond the usual justifications for their program. We agree with them that inflation must be curbed. We agree with them that blacks do better when the economy is better. We agree with them that America must produce more and create more jobs in the private sector.

But what I hope they will tell us is: What are black and poor people supposed to do in the meantime?

Even the wildest optimist knows it will take years for the president's program to produce the prosperity he promises. What do we do until then? How do poor people survive without the basic programs they need until then? How do they take advantage of future opportunities when present training and education programs are cut, when despair replaces hope?

A true dialogue goes beyond simple slogans and partial truths. It cuts to the core of the issues. So if this administration is serious about engaging in a frank, open dialogue with us, will it tell this Urban League Annual Conference how the black poor are to survive in the interim?

Will it tell us how its program will bring equality to black people, when we have had far higher unemployment and far lower income than whites, even when times were good?

Will it tell us what we are to say to our poor black constituents when we go home to our 116 cities where misery lies thick on the ground and the weeds of despair flourish?

The black community today feels itself under siege. We are victimized by the budget cuts. We are harassed by attacks on affirmative action. We are alarmed that state legislatures will redistrict our representatives out of the Congress and out of local offices. We are outraged by the administration's tilt toward racist South Africa. We are threatened by block grants.

And we are burdened by events beyond the political arena: by growing racial insensitivity and rising antiblack attitudes; by the murders of black children in Atlanta and violence against blacks elsewhere; by the continued deterioration of black neighborhoods; by the flow of drugs and the increase of crime; and by the rise of the fanatics of the far right like the Klan and the Nazis.

High on our long list of concerns is the future of the Voting Rights Act. It expires next year. Voting is, in President Reagan's words, "the most sacred right of free men and women." That sacred right will be lost to millions of black and Hispanic people unless the president comes out forcefully in favor of extending the Voting Rights Act. And we urge him in this conference to do so and to do it now.

The fight for voting rights symbolizes the erosion of black gains. We are now fighting the fight we fought sixteen years ago. And in some ways, we are dealing with basic issues like better race relations that were issues of the 1950s. We moved far beyond that stage, and now we are thrust back to square one.

But the path of progress has always been crooked and twisted. It has always been marked by two steps forward and one step backward. We cannot give way to despair; rather we must mobilize the black community to protect its rights and to prepare for the next push forward on the hard, rocky road to equality.

In many ways, today's challenges are more difficult. The national consensus for racial justice has withered.

For the complexities of today's racial, economic, and political issues are such that there is no one grand strategy or leader to deliver us. We will have to draw on our immense resources of survival skills to get us through these hard times. And we will have to cultivate our bonds of unity to once again overcome.

In many ways, it is back to basics for black people. That means a recommitment to the slow, agonizing work of building community strengths and community institutions.

The progress we have achieved has been due to the institutions rooted in our communities and responsive to our needs. Throughout history, it has been our churches, our press, our colleges, our community organizations that have fought on our behalf.

So now is the time for us to shore up those institutions, to strengthen them and support them. We of the Urban League movement know we cannot be fully effective unless other community institutions are strong. In effect, the civil rights movement is as strong as its weakest link, and each of us must cooperate and work together, while performing the roles and functions best suited to us.

Back to basics also means a recommitment to group progress. We reject completely the notion that individual progress is meaningful while half of our black brothers and sisters are mired in ghetto poverty. We reject completely the notion that a black person who has worked and clawed his way into the middle class has no responsibility to the black poor. And we reject just as completely the vile notion that a black person who has gained a toehold in America's middle class has anything to apologize for.

We are sick and tired of hardworking black people having to apologize for sharing the American Dream of a decent standard of living; of having to apologize for not being poor; of having to apologize for aspiring and achieving; of being put on a guilt trip for trying to make it.

We will not allow ourselves to be held hostage to other people's ideas about what our proper place is. We know that if you are black in America, you are in trouble; you are not safe, you are always in danger of losing the little you have. We know what it is to be poor; most of us are the first generation to be educated and to wear a white collar to work. All of us are bound by ties of family and racial unity to all black people.

Back to basics also means a recommitment to excellence. There is no margin granted to black Americans—we've got to be better than others in order to get what other Americans take for granted. That spirit of excellence and accomplishment must be characteristic of all our institutions. That spirit must be transmitted to our young people. The spirit of excellence can be the spark that revitalizes our communities.

Back to basics also means political action. It's hard to break through the cynicism that grips people who have been subjected to brutalizing poverty and hopelessness. But the 1980s must be the decade of maximizing black political strength. We have the numbers to influence events, but in election after election we throw away half our power by not voting. So citizenship education and political involvement in all parties must be a major priority in the 1980s.

Back to basics also means building coalitions. We've got to reach across class and ethnic lines to win victories for all people. America's tragedy is the racism that drives a wedge between whites and blacks who have so much to gain by working together.

Back to basics also means devising new strategies, alternatives for a nation that thinks old ideas that led to the Great Depression are new ideas for an uncertain future; alternatives like the Urban League's income-maintenance plan.

Back to basics also means challenging America's institutions. It means challenging the administration and the Congress to discover compassion, to make their conservatism humane. It means challenging the private sector to live up to its job creation and affirmative action obligations. It means challenging the churches to practice the morality they preach. It means challenging weak-kneed liberals and hard-hearted conservatives wherever they may be found. It means reminding America's institutions that black people are Americans, too, that our blood, sweat, and tears helped make this country what it is, and all we want is our fair share.

And back to basics means back to protesting our condition. Protest has been the basic response of black Americans, from the protest of the slave revolts to the protest of the March on Washington.

Now, when all about us is dark with despair, now is the time to raise high a fresh banner of protest. Now is the time to speak out loud and clear. Now is the time to tell the administration that poor people can't live on a diet of jelly beans, to tell local officials they can't close our hospitals, to tell corporations they can't hire us last and fire us first, to tell the school boards they are failing their duty to our children, to tell all of America's institutions that they must root out the racism at the core of our national life.

It was a black preacher right here in Washington, D.C., Francis Grimke,* who said many years ago:

> It is our duty to keep up the agitation of our rights, not only for our sakes, but for the sake of the nation at large. It would not only be against our own interest not to do so, but it would be unpatriotic for us quietly to acquiesce in the present condition of things, for it is a wrong condition of things. If justice sleeps in this land, let it not be because we have helped to lull it to sleep by our silence, our indifference; let it not be from lack of effort on our part to arouse it from its slumbers.

---

* Francis Grimke, pastor of the city's Fifteenth Street Presbyterian Church for nearly fifty years, was born into a family that included slave owners as well as abolitionists. He played a prominent role in the Niagara Movement and the founding of the NAACP.

That is our duty, to our nation, to ourselves, to our children, and to our children's children. Let us then get back to the basic job of building new foundations for a new thrust for equality. Let us get back to the basic job of making America *America* again—this time for everyone!

As we do our duty, let us remember that dark midnights, hard and difficult times, a perilous future adversity at every turn are nothing new to us. We been here before. Our load has never been easy. So walk together children and don'tcha get weary. We've come this far by faith. Our case is just.

So as we confront a new administration and a new mood, the attitude of black people and the Urban League is summed up in a song that says:

> *I don't feel no ways tired,*
> *I've come too far from where I started from,*
> *Nobody told me that the road would be easy,*
> *I don't believe He brought me this far to leave me.**

With that faith, with that hope, let this conference begin.

---

* Lyrics by the Reverend Dr. James Cleveland (1931–1991), a celebrated minister, as well as a producer and performer of gospel music.

OUR CHILDREN, OUR PEERS

1981

In the fall of 1980, I got a call from Martin Meyerson, the president of the University of Pennsylvania, where my daughter, Vickee, was a senior. "I've got you trapped now in a situation you cannot refuse, Vernon," he said, and I could feel the triumphant glee in his voice. "The trustees (of the university) have voted to have you as our commencement speaker this year and to give you an honorary degree. And since your daughter is graduating, you can't be anywhere else that day."

I calmly said, "Martin, speak to Vickee, and I'll do whatever she wants." I knew that Vickee's thoughts about my being a public figure at her school ceremonies were complex. I had spoken at Vickee's graduation from elementary school and at her graduation from high school, and I suspected she might be thinking: Enough is enough. And when Vickee talked with Meyerson, she said she preferred that I not speak at commencement. When she came home at Thanksgiving, she explained that she'd found herself thinking, "Why can't my daddy be an ordinary daddy and sit in the stands like all the other daddys?"

I said, "That's fine with me. Whatever you want," and I thought no more about it until the Christmas holidays when Vickee was home again. It was late in the evening. Vickee had gone out with friends, and I sat in the living room of our apartment on Fifth Avenue, smoking a cigar, sipping a glass of brandy, and looking at the snow falling on Central Park. When she returned, Vickee walked over to me and said that she had decided I should give the commencement address at her graduation, after all. I asked her why she had changed her mind, and she replied, "Because I've decided that you're not an ordinary daddy."

We hugged and shared a tear together, and as a result, I gave the most important commencement address of my life.

UNIVERSITY OF PENNSYLVANIA

Philadelphia, Pennsylvania

May 18, 1981

*M*ost commencement addresses remind me of the French philosopher who said that "people propose to us patterns of life which neither the proposer nor his hearers have any hope of following, or, what is more, any desire to follow."

So I won't exhort today. Nor will I do what I have been doing for many weeks now—making speeches suggesting that the surgeon-general issue a warning that the administration's budget is dangerous to the health of poor people and minority people.

Instead, I want to talk on a more personal level. I want to talk about the joys and the heartaches, the pleasures and the fears, of raising children and seeing them one day as full-grown adults, graduates of a great university.

For that is the position in which I find myself today: That is the reason this day, so special for you, is also so special for me. Among the graduates today is my daughter, Vickee. That is what makes today so special, so different.

When a man's only child graduates from college, his mind runs along the course of time until it arrives at the beginnings: the joyful news that a child is on the way, the long months of anxious waiting, the shared experience of expectant parents.

I think back to the rush to the hospital, the pacing of the corridors, and finally the wonderful news that unto us a child is born, a baby girl, a fresh breeze of future gladness and promise.

I vividly remember looking through the window at my newborn baby in those early-morning hours so long ago. And I remember my feeling of joyous excitement, waving frantically at that tiny bundle whose eyes were closed tightly, whose little body was exhausted with the effort of coming into this world.

Your parents will recall their similar experience when you were born. And they may also have felt what I felt at that time, amid the joy and excitement a faint feeling of disquiet; a twinge of anxiety about the question marks in life that await our children.

At the root of that feeling lay the limitless potentials symbolized by the awesome experience of birth. The writer John Agee put it so well:

In every child who is born, under no matter what circumstances, and of no matter what parents, the potentiality of
the human race is born again; and in him, too, once more,
and of each of us, our terrific responsibility towards human life; towards the utmost idea of goodness, of the horror of error, and of God.

That feeling never leaves parents. Before us always are the
question marks of the future; the uncertainties of life that can
creep up unawares and lift our dreams high or turn them into
nightmares. Yes, that anxiety is always present—always making
us try harder for our children's sakes, always making us aware of
their needs and guarding their futures.

Our children grow. We count each new development as land-
marks in our personal histories: the day our baby takes the first
step, speaks her first word, goes off to school for the first time.

We watched our children grow, and we grew with them. We
stayed up nights when they were sick, and we tended their cuts
and bruises. We had good days; we had bad days. We made mis-
takes, and hurt them in ways grown-ups can never comprehend.
But we also made them happy, joining in their gay laughter on a
summer's afternoon.

And as they grew older, we shared their new experiences. We
tried to remember the little math we learned and the history we
forgot, because they needed our help with homework. We laid
down the law, and then compromised. We fought over staying
out late, or the boys that turned up on our doorstep, or the clut-
ter in the room.

Sometimes our children were rebellious and wrong. Sometimes we parents were dogmatic and wrong. Sometimes we gave our children the comfort they needed, and then, as time passed, they gave us comfort in our bad moments. Sometimes that is when the turning point comes, when the dependency shifts. For so many years I lent my daughter what strength I had, and last summer, in my time of trial and pain, it was she who brought strength to me; she who brought me the power of love and will to help me pull through.

Finally, the day comes when our children are no longer children. That is why Commencement Day is so important. It is a rite of passage, a formal declaration of independence, a passing over into the larger world.

"Commencement" seems a strange term to use for a ceremony that *ends* the years of college. But it is very apt. For "commencement" means a beginning, and this day signifies not so much the end of one's college career but the beginning of one's adult life.

This day marks the cutting of the strings, the leaving of a protected environment for the larger world. It marks a fundamental change in our relations with our children. For they are now our peers.

They have their own lives to lead; their own dreams to follow; their own aspirations to seek.

Before, we parents were center stage. Now we are in the wings, pushed back by the inevitable passage of time and circumstance, pushed back as we ourselves once pushed back our own parents, and they, theirs.

So we parents, who have spent the past two decades learning and adjusting to new situations and new phases of development, must now adjust to yet another phase, perhaps the most difficult of all to accept. But our acceptance of this new order is a mark of our own maturity, and a final service to the children we love so dearly—the gift of allowing them to be themselves.

Thus far I have been talking to your parents, to my fellow fathers and mothers of this graduating class. But this is your day, and I do want to say a few things to you directly.

The first is to apologize for the world into which you graduate. It is, in many ways, a mean world. The superpowers rattle rockets at each other. Television brings us, between commercials for expensive cars and clothing, pictures of some of the earth's starving millions. People still judge other people by the color of their skin. Pockets of hate pollute our human environment. Right here, in the shadow of this great university, well over one out of five black people are out of work.

Yes, it is in many ways, a mean, mean world. But it is not much different from the world we entered. And in some ways it is a better world. When I returned home after my college graduation, it was to separate drinking fountains, the back of the bus, and the denial of basic constitutional rights.

So the world has changed. Not nearly enough, but it has changed. And it changed because in the midst of that meanness, buried deep within the caves of injustice, there was the throbbing of the human spirit, the determination by millions of individuals that wrong is something to overcome, not to tolerate.

And so many wrongs were overcome. The many that remain are ours—together—to overcome. But the prime responsibility must be yours, for you enter this brave new world unscarred by the battles we have fought, undaunted by the obstacles we have faced, and unburdened by the many myths we were taught to believe.

Your commencement marks the beginnings of your acceptance of what Agee called "the terrific responsibility toward human life."

You now share that responsibility fully. You are adults. You are our peers. From today onward, you will shape your own lives and your own destinies.

And you will help shape our nation's destiny—and the world's. I ask you to give to your children a better world than we give to you. I ask you to temper your striving for material success, for the glitter of things, with the drive to overcome the injustice and misery that still stalk our nation and our planet.

I ask you to remember the words of the poet who wrote:

> *I am only one,*
> *But still I am one.*
> *I cannot do everything.*
> *But still I can do something.*
> *And because I cannot do everything,*
> *I will not refuse to do the something that I can do.**

---

* Edward Everett Hale (1822–1909) was a Unitarian minister, orator, and statesman.

To you, our children, our adult peers and partners in uncharted paths, we, your parents, are proud of you. We love you. And as you go down from this place, as you say farewell to your alma mater, be steadfast, be strong, be of good cheer and, as my friend Ossie Davis is fond of saying, may your own dreams be your only boundaries henceforth, now, and forever.

BAD FIX IN AMERICA

The Reagan Years

1983

"We're in a bad fix in America when eight evil old men and one vain and foolish woman can speak a verdict on American liberties. Our nation from this day forward is no better than Russia insofar as expecting the blessings of God is concerned. You no longer live in a nation that is religiously free."

So said Reverend Bob Jones III, president of the fundamentalist Christian Bob Jones University, on May 24, 1983, to students gathered in Greenville, South Carolina, at the school's mandatory daily chapel meeting. Jones's denunciation of the U.S. Supreme Court followed the Court's affirmation that the Internal Revenue Service was right to deny the university a tax exemption because of its racially discriminatory policies. Bob Jones University, which had been founded in 1927 and had only begun admitting black students in the 1970s, barred students from interracial dating and marriage. The Court's decision also barred granting a tax exemption to the Goldsboro Christian Schools, of Goldsboro, North Carolina,

which did not admit blacks at all. Both claimed a literal interpretation of the Bible as justification for their racism.

The Reverend Jerry Falwell, a founder of the right-wing
political action group the Moral Majority and head of his
own fundamentalist Christian university in Virginia, sec-
onded Jones's sentiments. He called the Court's 8–1 ruling "a
blow against religious liberty."

The decision provoked quite a different response elsewhere. At the Department of Justice, for example, according
to an account in the *New York Times*, a large contingent of
the civil rights division's career attorneys "greeted the ruling
with backslapping elation." What made their reaction so
noteworthy was that they were cheering the Supreme Court's
having dealt the administration of Ronald Reagan a deeply
embarrassing defeat.

There is no better illustration than the Bob Jones case of
the Reagan administration's deliberate, cavalier disregard of
hard-won federal civil rights policies and its, at best, indifference to aiding black Americans' advancement into society's
mainstream. As the Court's vote indicated—Justice William
Rehnquist registered the only dissent—the matter of barring
tax exemptions for schools with racist policies and practices
was settled law. Indeed, when it became clear in 1981 that the
Bob Jones case would reach the Supreme Court, the Justice
Department readied itself to defend the government's anti-
discrimination position, which was based on a 1970 IRS ruling. Instead, in January 1982, President Reagan issued a

stunning statement. He declared that the government's authority to invoke the regulation was actually invalid. The administration had no choice but to grant Bob Jones University
the exemption.

The reversal provoked a torrent of scorn throughout the
country, and even within the government itself. More than
100 of the 175 career attorneys in the Justice Department's
civil rights division signed a letter protesting the administration's new position. The staff of the U.S. Solicitor General's
Office, the government's lawyers in cases before the Supreme
Court, in effect refused to represent the White House. Reagan appointee William Bradford Reynolds, the assistant attorney general for civil rights who crafted much of the
administration's anti–civil rights positions throughout the
1980s, argued the case before the Court.

Because the White House had now abandoned the government's previous position, the Supreme Court appointed a
private attorney to defend the IRS regulation and its choice
was instructive: William T. Coleman, Jr., who had served as
secretary of transportation under President Gerald Ford, was
a widely respected pillar of the establishment. But he also
had impeccable civil rights credentials. As a young lawyer, he
had been part of the legal team Thurgood Marshall brought
together to prepare the *Brown v. Board of Education* cases,
and he was at that time chairman of the organization Marshall had led—the NAACP Legal Defense and Educational
Fund, Inc. (LDF).

The administration's support for Bob Jones University—
its attempt to renew government support for racist policies—
was blatant but not inexplicable. It was rooted most directly
in its efforts to please South Carolina senator Strom Thurmond, the erstwhile Democrat who had switched to the Republican Party in the 1960s when Presidents Kennedy and
Johnson committed their party to fully support civil rights
for blacks. In 1982, Thurmond was not only chairman of the
powerful Senate Judiciary Committee. He was also a trustee
of Bob Jones University.

But the administration's gambit had a far broader purpose
than just lending government support to two schools. For
one thing, by the early 1980s there were more than 100 white
private schools in the South that had lost or been denied tax
exemptions by the IRS because they had refused to adopt
nondiscriminatory policies. The Reagan rule reversal was intended to benefit them, too. In that regard, then, it was a key
plank of what I described in this speech as the Reagan counterrevolution: "the deliberate, conscious, and willful attempt
to roll back the Second Reconstruction," which the civil
rights movement of the 1950s and 1960s had brought about.

The day after the Court delivered its decision, a *New York
Times* editorial succinctly represented the widespread sentiment. "President Reagan and the lawyers he put in charge of
protecting civil rights should stand ashamed," it declared.
"Racial hatred is not tax exempt, the Supreme Court ruled
yesterday by a lopsided vote. Only this administration—and

one dissenting justice—ever doubted it. . . . Mr. Reagan's reaction yesterday was to say 'We will obey the law.' It's about
time."

But despite the victory in the Bob Jones case, by early 1983
there were plenty of indications—some emanating from the
White House, some from the society at large—that made it
clear it was black America that was in a "bad fix."

Broad-scale economic forces—such as the decline in manufacturing jobs and the development of the technologically
driven information society, which demanded workers have
more education and definite skills—continued to undermine
the fortunes of the segment of black Americans at the bottom of the socioeconomic ladder. Even as more and more
blacks were benefiting from the expansion of opportunity the
civil rights victories had produced, the scope of the problems
haunting the black poor remained striking.

Blacks' overall predicament was sharply exacerbated by the
Reagan administration's actions and pronouncements.
Throughout 1982 and 1983, the president opposed the congressional bill establishing a federal holiday honoring Martin
Luther King, Jr., despite the substantial bipartisan support it
had. He signed the legislation in November 1983 only because it was clear that there were more than enough votes in
Congress to override his threatened veto. But his insinuation
that King was a tool of Communists—a charge standard
among whites who had opposed the civil rights movement—
was for many blacks unforgivable.

Reagan also initially opposed extending the Voting Rights Act of 1965, which was up for renewal in 1982, and unsuccessfully tried to dilute the act's provisions. Only because he faced support for renewal in Congress did Reagan reluctantly sign a strengthened version of the bill. In every area of government where blacks showed a significant group interest—from speaking out forcefully against the South African government policy of apartheid to slashing funds from federal civil rights enforcement agencies and offices—the Reagan administration's attitude toward black America was clear and devastating.

I felt I had to speak out, a feeling that crystallized when I was invited to give the Samuel Rubin Lecture at Columbia Law School in March 1983. This was to be my first public-speaking engagement in the two years since I had retired from the National Urban League and become a senior partner at the law firm of Akin, Gump, Strauss, Hauer & Feld. I was no longer a "black leader." I led no black organization. I spoke for no formal "black" constituency. Now, I spoke only for myself. But some number of people within black America and in the larger society believed that I still had some things to say about racial and other issues worth their attention.

Speaking to the law students at Columbia provided an ideal venue for setting out on this new stage of my life as a public speaker. Before me was an audience of some of the sharpest minds of the new generation—mostly, but not all American, and of a great mix of racial, ethnic, and religious backgrounds—most of whom knew of the black freedom struggle of the 1950s and 1960s only through the books they had read. They had come of age in a period of reaction, when many were dismissing the civil rights era as "the past." It was my responsibility to tell them of the past—particularly the past I had witnessed and participated in and analyzed—and make clear to them two main things. One was that the events of the past were not irrelevant in the present, but instead were a powerful force. A knowledge and appreciation of the past made it possible to summon up the power to provoke the same feeling that had fueled the heroic black struggles of the 1950s and 1960s. In Reagan's America there was an urgent need to explain that all was not well, and that a new generation needed to summon the inspiration to set it aright.

COLUMBIA UNIVERSITY SCHOOL OF LAW
New York, New York
March 2, 1983

*T*homas Jefferson once said, "It is the trade of lawyers to question everything, yield nothing, and to talk by the hour." Today, I want to bear out at least some of Jefferson's statement. I would like to question some assumptions about civil rights progress and about our nation's policies. I will yield nothing to the current mythology that says the civil rights revolution fulfilled its aims and that the Great Society programs failed. I will, however, promise not to talk for more than an hour.

It is a mistake to view the civil rights movement of the 1960s as a self-enclosed entity. Rather, it must be seen as part of the continuum in the black struggle for freedom. That struggle began with revolts on board slave ships in the seventeenth century, continued with slave revolts and passive resistance to the slave system of the eighteenth century, sparked the abolitionist movement, led to the Civil War, and continues to this day.

In this process, the struggle evolved in the 1960s to the point where it captured the imagination and the conscience of the nation, overturned the segregation system of the South, and forever changed the legal status of black citizens. This revolution met its end in the 1970s, which saw the erosion of some of its gains. And in the 1980s, it faces a full-blown counterrevolution in the form of Reaganism.

Today, I want to talk a bit about that revolution and the counterrevolution it faces, no longer from the vantage point of an active combatant but as an interested observer with a personal stake in black equality, as an American citizen with a stake in the fulfillment of America's ideals, and as a practicing lawyer with a stake in the achievement of a system both fair and just.

The thrust for civil rights cannot be regarded purely as a drive to assure equal treatment under the Constitution. It very quickly became enmeshed in the quest for social and economic equality as well. Abstract legal rights were essential to the movement. Without them, blacks would have been condemned to a perpetual apartheid, forever barred from socioeconomic equality.

But once the issues moved away from the purely legal, once they moved from the abstract right to register at a hotel to the real-world issue of the opportunity to earn the money to pay the hotel bill, the consensus in favor of equality faded away.

The process was described by Martin Luther King, Jr., just before he was killed. "Negroes became outraged by blatant inequality," he said.

> Their ultimate goal was total, unqualified freedom. The majority of white progressives were outraged by the brutality displayed. Their goal was improvement or limited progression. Obtaining the right to use public facilities, register and vote, token educational advancement, brought to the Negro a sense of achievement; he felt the momentum. But it brought to the whites a sense of completion. When Negroes assertively moved on to ascend the second rung of the ladder, a firm resistance from the white community became manifest.

Let us take a closer look at the civil rights revolution of the 1960s, which I will refer to as the "Second Reconstruction." The period shares many features of the Reconstruction era of the late 1860s and early 1870s, and the term "Second Reconstruction" is flexible enough to include both the thrust for civil rights and the socioeconomic issues that are inseparable from that thrust.

During both periods, blacks made rapid advances, had considerable white support, benefited from laws assuring their rights, faced violence from racists bound to uphold the old order. In both cases, once concrete steps began to be taken so that it was not simply stark legal pronouncements but also practical and concrete results that began to be achieved, the nation had serious second thoughts. In the first Reconstruction those second thoughts won out; almost all the practical progress was lost, and blacks were left with the empty statement of the legal principles of the Thirteenth, Fourteenth, and Fifteenth Amendments. As Justice Fortas would later point out, for decades the Fourteenth Amendment was primarily used to guarantee the rights of railroads.

To a large extent, the triumphs of the Second Reconstruction lay in the process of defining, conferring, and implementing black citizens' rights, rights that had been freely granted to white citizens. The question now is whether after this new period of defining rights—largely analogous to that great legal advance after the Civil War—the nation will again turn away from the great practical steps that are necessary to implement those rights in concrete and meaningful ways.

This process of defining, conferring, and implementing rights was part of an effort that had been mushrooming for years. Judicial decisions had begun to undermine the legal underpinnings of the system of segregation. Federal courts had outlawed the white primary system and state-segregated professional schools. After World War II, the armed services had been desegregated by presidential executive order. In the celebrated *Brown* decision of 1954, the Supreme Court declared public school segregation unconstitutional.

But these and other holes drilled in the armor of segregation still left the system largely intact. As the South entered the 1960s, its schools were still segregated, *Brown* notwithstanding; its laws still denied equal treatment to blacks; and its customs, buttressed by those laws, still enforced black separation.

Dismantling that structure of segregation took a mixture of executive orders, judicial decisions, and laws. Allow me a brief moment to sketch in a few of the most prominent of those.

In 1962, President Kennedy signed Executive Order 11063, prohibiting discrimination based on race, color, creed, or national origin in housing or related facilities receiving federal assistance. In 1965, Executive Order 11246 required federal contractors to eliminate employment discrimination and required affirmative action to provide equal employment opportunity. And in 1969, Executive Order 11478 submitted federal agencies to the same mandate.

The Supreme Court issued literally dozens of decisions extending the constitutional rights of black citizens. Some of those key decisions, like the *Brown* decision, came in the 1950s. But some of the most important continued well into the 1970s.

The Court did more than simply uphold challenges to the constitutionality of the civil rights laws and executive orders of the sixties. It recognized the need to achieve results. It ratified the use of busing to desegregate unconstitutionally segregated school systems. It barred non-job-related tests and practices that excluded disproportionate numbers of minorities from the workplace. It upheld voluntary affirmative action plans and federal set-asides for minority businesses. And, in 1968, it even revived the Civil Rights Act of 1866, proving that the law sleeps but does not die.

But the Court, like the nation, also retreated in the 1970s. While denying any retreat in principle, recent decisions were equivocal on affirmative action and on standards of proof of discrimination. And the Court has trimmed back its commitment to some remedies for unconstitutionally segregated school systems.

We are perhaps most familiar with the laws that form the backbone of the Second Reconstruction: the Civil Rights Act of 1964, the Voting Rights Act of 1965, the Fair Housing Act of 1968, and numerous, lesser-known laws that prohibited discrimination in a variety of federally funded programs and required affirmative action programs.

These executive orders, judicial decisions, and laws effectively dismantled a system that had been intact since the end of the first Reconstruction.

But it must be understood that this revolution was not from the top down; it did not occur because national leadership suddenly decided to implement the Constitution. Rather, it responded to a mass movement whose advantage lay in direct confrontation with a legal and social system that was morally indefensible, socially backward, and economically counterproductive.

Black people in the 1960s toppled segregation themselves— through black organization, black demonstrations, black sacrifices, and by the blood, sweat, and tears of black people and committed whites. Civil rights were not granted in Washington, they were won by the Freedom Riders, by the marchers on the road from Selma to Montgomery, by heroic black people who were beaten senseless because they refused to move from a lunch counter until they were served, and by ordinary black people who refused to ride the buses in Montgomery until they were allowed to sit anywhere on those buses.

And black people in the 1960s were aided by white allies. Countless white people were as repelled by the indignities faced by Southern blacks. Those allies were valuable—they marched with us; they fought side by side with us; some even died with us.

Ironically, perhaps the most valuable involuntary allies were the Bull Connors and the Jim Clarks—the sheriffs who clubbed peaceful demonstrators and who turned fire hoses on little schoolchildren marching for human dignity. The television cameras brought that sorry spectacle into every home in the country. And even those who had little sympathy for the plight of black people recognized the moral imperative of wiping out overt, legal segregation.

By the mid–1960s, the legal structure of segregation was ended. Black people enjoyed the protection of the federal government's implementation of their constitutional rights.

It is hard for us, in the midst of the counterrevolution of the 1980s, to fully appreciate what that meant for millions of black people. But we can capture just a hint of its meaning by the true story of a ninety-two-year-old black man who registered to vote just days after passage of the Voting Rights Act in 1965. He was one of literally hundreds of black people in Marengo County, Alabama, who turned out to exercise their democratic, constitutional right to vote for the first time.

When that old man, dressed in his Sunday best, reached the registration official's desk, the federal examiner asked him: "Why didn't you ever register before?"

And the old man answered: "I never believed in putting myself in the way of trouble-a-comin.'"

He was then asked: "Why are you here now, after ninety-two years?" And he responded: "I am here today after ninety-two years 'cause trouble ain't-a-comin' like it used to did."

The fear that was lifted from that old man's shoulders, and from the shoulders of millions of other black people, marked a new step toward freedom for all Southerners—black and white.

The Second Reconstruction finally brought the South into the union. It democratized political life, civilized social life, and gave new vigor to economic life. Without the Second Reconstruction, a Southerner could not have become president and the Cotton Belt could not have become the Sun Belt.

The economic level of the Second Reconstruction is something too often neglected. It is forgotten that the 1963 march on Washington was for "jobs and freedom." We may have started by marching for the right to sit in the front of the bus, but the movement quickly encompassed such issues as whether blacks will be hired to drive the bus and help manage the system of public transportation.

That is why the Great Society programs cannot be separated from the steps taken to define and confer constitutional rights. For those programs were necessary to implement those rights and to draw black citizens into the mainstream of national life.

It seems to me a fairly obvious conclusion to draw, but this simple point apparently escapes the understanding of the president of the United States. Several months ago, President Reagan addressed a meeting of black Republicans and told them that black people would have been better off if the Great Society had never existed. All those programs, he said, just made government grow, consumed tax dollars, and—quote—"threatened the character of our people"—end quote.

The irony here is that the Great Society and the Second Reconstruction of which it was an integral part, made that meeting possible. It was the Civil Rights Act of 1964 that gave those black Republicans he was talking to the right to meet in a downtown hotel. It was the Voting Rights Act of 1965 that gave them the right to register and vote. It was the Fair Housing Act of 1968 that gave them the right to buy houses in the suburbs. It was the laws, judicial decisions, and executive orders on affirmative action that helped get those black Republicans jobs in government and in corporate America, jobs that had been closed to earlier generations of blacks.

And it was the Great Society programs that cut black poverty in half. Food stamps fed the hungry. Head Start and education aid helped bring our kids the schooling they had been denied. Legal aid gave poor people a stake in the system of justice. The Job Corps took kids off the street and put them into jobs. Medicare and Medicaid helped old people and poor people get decent health care.

The spokesmen for the mean society say the Great Society made people dependent. The truth is that the Great Society programs helped bring to the most disadvantaged the education and the skills to compete in the job market. It helped them achieve basic survival needs denied them by the operations of an imperfect market system.

We see the results of the Great Society programs today: in the marked improvement in reading test scores among black children in poor neighborhoods, in longer black life expectancy, in black sheriffs and mayors, and in campaigns by George Wallace or Strom Thurmond in black precincts.

The problems with the Great Society were not that they made us dependent or enlarged government, but that they were too limited, were underfunded, and too short-lived to amount to more than a beginning.

Senator Daniel Moynihan, who served under both Lyndon Johnson and Richard Nixon, has written: "The social reforms of the mid-decade had been oversold, and with the coming of the war, underfinanced to the degree that seeming failure could be as-cribed almost to intent."

The War on Poverty amounted to little more than a skirmish. It gave way to the real war—the war in Vietnam—which increas-ingly absorbed America's resources and energies.

If the Second Reconstruction did not achieve its goals of racial equality and an end to poverty, it did leave a lasting, positive mark on America and its people.

First, it restored the rule of law and the rule of the Constitution to the South—with far-reaching social and economic results.

Second, it enlarged personal freedom and civil liberties for all, and most especially for black citizens whose constitutional rights had been persistently violated.

Third, it increased the empowerment of the disadvantaged, significantly expanding black political power.

Fourth, it altered the structure of the black community by fostering the creation of a new leadership class made up of officeholders, corporate managers, and professionals. The black community became more pluralistic as it edged closer to participation in mainstream America.

Fifth, it brought about a lasting change in the way black people saw themselves and the society. The experience of overthrowing segregation and of sharing power, however limited, resulted in a self-confident assertiveness that will never be lost.

Sixth, it brought extraordinary economic gains to the black community. Black poverty was down sharply, and black income, black educational achievement, and black occupational status were up.

Seventh, it brought similar gains to the white poor. For all the stigma attached to the poverty programs as "black" programs, they were inaugurated (in part) as a response to white poverty in Appalachia and wound up benefiting far more whites than blacks.

Finally, the Second Reconstruction brought the nation to a new, higher level of civility. It brought America closer to its stated ideals and principles. Americans felt better about themselves and about their country; they felt morally renewed. Pride replaced shame, and a sense of accomplishment replaced apathy.

Just as the Second Reconstruction must be seen as part of a continuum in the black struggle for equality, so, too, must its end be seen as part of the continuum of white resistance to equality.

If I had to pin a date on just when the Second Reconstruction ended, I would choose the election of 1968, in which Richard

Nixon defeated Hubert Humphrey. Nixon won, in part, because of a failure of nerve among liberals. Determined to punish Humphrey for his loyalty to Johnson's war policy, many either did not vote or voted for the far more hawkish Nixon.

They were right about the war. But they were wrong about Humphrey. Instead of ending the moral disaster of the Vietnam War, they helped end the moral triumph of the Second Reconstruction. Instead of punishing Humphrey, they punished the white and black poor whose gains were imperiled.

American liberalism has been marked by a lack of staying power. Liberals swung from the quest for black equality to ending the war in Vietnam to saving the environment to backing women's rights, and now, to fighting for a nuclear freeze. What will tomorrow's fashionable issue be?

Liberals also suffer from a disease known as "There's no difference"—as in there is no difference between Carter and Reagan. The mixture of absolutist political judgments and short attention spans has been American liberalism's fatal flaw.

There were, of course, other reasons for the end of the Second Reconstruction. The war in Vietnam proved the unalterable truth that a nation cannot have both guns and butter. Resources that could have rebuilt our cities were used to destroy rice paddies.

And once the major thrust of black efforts turned from winning rights on paper to implementing those rights, white support melted away. It was one thing to support integrated lunch counters in South Carolina, quite another to support integrated schools in Chicago.

As black demands moved north, our former supporters spiritually moved south. "No, not one" became the battle cry not only of the governor of Alabama but of whites resisting school desegregation in Boston and of whites resisting housing desegregation in New York.

I should also mention the negative effects of a black power movement that encouraged self-isolation while frightening away some white allies. A similar effect was produced by the urban riots of the late sixties, riots that occurred mainly in the North, where blacks did not share in the gains made by Southerners.

The Second Reconstruction had not yet adequately addressed the core issues of concern to Northern blacks—grinding poverty, subtle discrimination, police brutality, lack of opportunity, and more. Events in the South fueled their expectations; failure to meet those expectations fueled their frustration.

Thus, by the end of the 1960s, black people were suspended in midair—with new empowerments and new opportunities on the one hand, but still on the margins of society and vulnerable to sharp setbacks on the other.

By fostering an atmosphere of racial suspicion by abandoning key reforms and by demonstrating its insensitivity to black concerns, the Nixon administration helped bury the Second Reconstruction. Where Kennedy and Johnson had lent their prestige and power to the cause of black equality, Richard Nixon lent his to the cause of legitimizing a status quo that left blacks still disadvantaged, still victimized, and still far from America's mainstream.

Exhausted by a decade of rapid social change, divided by the war in Vietnam, and disillusioned by Watergate, Americans turned inward. A series of recessions burst upon a troubled nation, undermining America's self-confidence and its idealism. In a stagnant economy, those who had become more selfish than those who had not, became more despairing.

The withering away of the Second Reconstruction can be measured by the widening gap between whites and blacks. The National Urban League's recent report, "The State of Black America, 1983," documents the perilous state of the black community.

Some blacks have made it. *Some* blacks are now partially absorbed into the mainstream of American society. But the bulk of black Americans are locked into socioeconomic conditions only few whites have tasted. Let me give you just a few of the facts that document the racial nature of their disadvantage:

+ Life expectancy for blacks trails that for whites. Life expectancy for black males today is 65.5 years, a point reached by white men in the mid–1940s. For black women, it is about 74 years, a point reached by white women back in 1950. Infant mortality is well over double the rate for whites.

+ Median income for blacks with some college education is lower than for white high school dropouts. At every level of educational achievement, blacks earn far less than whites.

◆ Black unemployment is at 21 percent, a figure not matched by whites since the early 1930s. Since the early seventies, black unemployment has been over double the white rate.

◆ For every $100 earned by the typical white family, the typical black family earns about $56. That's the lowest black-white income ratio since 1960, before the start of the Second Reconstruction. And it is a decline from 1970, when blacks had moved to 61 percent of white income.

The poverty rate among black families is over 31 percent, compared to under 9 percent for white families. Before the Second Reconstruction, almost half of all black families were poor; by the end of the sixties, black poverty had fallen to under 28 percent; now it is up again.

The basic thrust of the Second Reconstruction was to promote parity between blacks and whites—parity in law and in socioeconomic status. The brief decade of the sixties did produce rapid movement toward parity. The long decade of the seventies moved that goal further from view. And the counterrevolution of the eighties appears designed to remove the prospect of ultimate parity from the horizon.

Richard Nixon halted, but did not reverse, the Second Reconstruction. It took Ronald Reagan to inaugurate the counterrevolution: the deliberate, conscious, and willful attempt to roll back the Second Reconstruction.

In order to keep my promise to violate Jefferson's dictum that lawyers "talk by the hour," I will only sketch in a few of the indications that the Reagan counterrevolution amounts to a full-scale war on the principles of the Second Reconstruction.

The Second Reconstruction was based on the concept of integrating American society. The Reagan counterrevolution is based on resegregating society. To be sure, it does not say that is the goal, but as John Mitchell* used to say: "Watch what we do, not what we say."

And what this administration has done is to go to the courts to seek dismantling of both voluntary and involuntary school busing. It has deemphasized civil rights enforcement. It has mounted an attack on affirmative action. It has violated the clear intent of Congress by suspending regulations that prevented segregation academies from enjoying tax-exempt status. Its one accomplishment—signing the extension of the Voting Rights Act—was forced upon it after its attempts to weaken the bill failed.

The Second Reconstruction was about empowerment, about extending people's participation in decisions that affect them. From the Voting Rights Act through the community action programs of OEO [Office of Economic Opportunity], it brought some measure of power to the powerless.

---

* John Mitchell was Richard Nixon's acerbic attorney general—the first U.S. attorney general to be convicted of a crime and imprisoned. In 1975, he was convicted of conspiracy, obstruction of justice, and perjury for his role in the Watergate scandal that ultimately led to Nixon's resignation from office.

The Reagan counterrevolution operates to concentrate power among those that hold it—state and local power elites, the affluent, the business community. The most glaring example of its attempt to weaken the process of empowerment is the continuing struggle to destroy the Legal Services Corporation. The one federal program specifically designed to remove poverty as a barrier to participation in the legal system is marked for destruction. What the administration could not achieve through congressional action it has tried to accomplish through unqualified and unsympathetic appointees charged with destroying the program from within.

The Second Reconstruction was about democratizing economic life, tilting resources to those in need through programs providing survival assistance and programs that create opportunities for self-advancement.

The Reagan counterrevolution has ruthlessly cut those programs, inflicting fresh hardships on the poorest among us. It has withdrawn funds for education, job training, and job creation programs designed to help people to become independent earners. It presided over a combination of tax cuts and spending cuts that effectively transferred massive resources from the poor to the rich.

The Second Reconstruction was about using federal power and federal resources to extend constitutional rights and to create a more equitable socioeconomic system. It was a logical extension of the New Deal.

But the Reagan counterrevolution's Raw Deal seeks to shrink the size of the federal government by abandoning essential public services or by dispersing them to the states. The New Federalism amounts to a return to states' rights, a return to concentrating power among local elites.

The real issue behind the New Federalism is whether we are one people or fifty; whether poverty and discrimination are national issues or local; whether the general welfare will prevail over parochial local interests.

And behind the ideological combat over the concept of the New Federalism is the strategic one. By shifting social programs to the states, the Reagan counterrevolution would ensure that they ultimately wither away, caught in a squeeze between conflicting local needs and inadequate local resources.

With the Reagan counterrevolution, we have come full circle, from Lyndon Johnson's "We shall overcome" to Ronald Reagan's "We shall overthrow."

The lesson that many people are drawing from this counterrevolution is that the fates of blacks and whites are linked. Millions who voted for Reagan in the hope that he would end those so-called black programs, are today standing on welfare lines, registering for food stamps, and looking in vain for a job-training program to join.

The Reagan counterrevolution has integrated poverty to an extent not seen in five decades. Its radical economic theories have turned a recession into a depression. Its numbers never made sense. Any ten-year-old with a pocket calculator could have told them that you cannot cut taxes, raise defense spending, and slam the brakes on the money supply without incurring huge deficits and an economic depression.

The failure of Reaganomics has helped bring Americans back to their senses. They are beginning to understand that by trying to help blacks advance and by reducing the inequities in our system, the Second Reconstruction helped whites, too. And now they see that when the Reagan counterrevolution increases inequality and removes the helping hand extended to black people, whites are hurt as well.

There's no question that the counterrevolution has severely damaged black people, but it has also hit hard at millions of white people who never before had to worry about losing their job, losing their home, or feeding their kids. The victims of the new color-blind misery are the core of what has been called the New Poor—solid, respectable middle-class people now living in tent cities in Houston or in shelters in New York, standing in line for surplus cheese in thousands of church soup kitchens from coast to coast.

And among the majority relatively untouched by the negative effects of the Reagan counterrevolution, we see the beginnings of unease—the feeling that what has happened is not right, not fair, not just.

The Reagan counterrevolution contains within itself the seeds of its own destruction. By ignoring the realities of the world, it ensures that it will be incapable of dealing with the world. By basing policies on nostalgia for the good old days, it only re-creates the bad old days of the Great Depression. By counting on negative forces such as selfishness, greed, and racism, it has helped restore the spirit of those positive forces of compassion, fairness, and belief in an open, pluralistic, integrated society.

The impending defeat of the Reagan counterrevolution is inevitable, if only because the Second Reconstruction, like the New Deal, left a lasting impact on America. Its basic principles have become part of the structure of the way we think about our society. Aside from the radical right, Americans of all political persuasions recognize that the federal government has to play a major role in shaping the economy, in providing opportunities for the disadvantaged, and in making our society more just and fair.

America has changed, people's minds have changed. What was once considered normal is now beyond the bounds of decency. Americans may not love busing, but they hate tax exemptions for segregated academies. They may not like welfare, but they hate seeing the homeless poor wandering the streets. Racism may linger, but a return to Jim Crow is unthinkable.

And because of those changes in America, I see the seeds of a new coalition for decency and fairness being planted today, seeds that are nurtured in the harsh ground of unfair, insensitive government policies and economic hard times.

I see that emerging new coalition in every city, town, and hamlet of America. It is black and white, old and young, urban and rural, rich and poor, labor and management, Democrats and Republicans, liberals and conservatives. This coalition need not be narrowly partisan and ideologically pure. Consensus is not necessary on every issue. Nor does every member have to love one another. Rather, it is a coalition that understands:

+ mutuality of interests,
+ that it is working people who buy Fords and Chevys,

+ that just plain ordinary folk shop at Penney's and
  Sears,
+ that when we work we consume,
+ that when the interest rates are low, we borrow for
  a house and a car.

A new coalition for decency and fairness that understands that our wants and needs are plain and simple—a decent job at a decent wage, a little white house with green shutters and a white picket fence, a car in the garage, food in the fridge, beer in the cooler, a TV in the den, tuition for the children, two weeks at the beach, a fair pension, a quiet funeral, and a debt-free estate.

Reaganism takes America to the brink. And Americans look into the deep abyss into which it wants us to jump, and they are saying no. Americans resent being asked to choose between meanness and fairness, between an arms race and a food race, between a mean society and a Great Society, between prosperity for all or depression for all but the rich.

Given those choices, Reaganism will be just a passing mistake in the history of a nation's march toward equality and justice. And Ronald Reagan will be seen by historians as having performed the invaluable service of bringing meanness to the surface. Throughout the seventies, that meanness festered, poisoning national life. It took Reaganism to make that meanness a cardinal feature of national policy, exposing it to full view, thus creating the conditions for removing it from the body politic.

The president can perform a second historically valuable service to the nation by not running for reelection in 1984. By refusing to run again, he can save the Republican Party from a repetition of its twenty years in the political wilderness that began in 1932. By not running he can bring fresh options to the Republican Party, thus ensuring the health of the two-party system. And by not running he can transform the crucial election of 1984 from a referendum on failed policies to a search for new options in a changing world.

Whether Reagan runs or not, there is in America today a coalition for decency and fairness that can bind Americans together, a coalition in search of a leadership that can articulate and implement American ideals and values.

It is a coalition that must include the legal profession. Over a century ago, de Tocqueville observed that "it is at the bar or the bench that the American aristocracy is found." That is even more true today, when lawyers stand guard over the control panels of our society.

I cannot discuss the civil rights revolution and today's counter-revolution without some discussion of my profession's role as a barometer of American race relations.

It is sad to note that today's aristocrats of the law are almost as segregated as in de Tocqueville's time. If, as I have stated, the Second Reconstruction was about empowerment and participation, then we must sadly conclude that it has had less effect on the legal profession than on other sectors of American life. For the legal profession remains a fortress closed to most black aspirants to legal careers.

The legal profession is the one profession in America that is inseparable from the system itself. Racial exclusion in the practice of law amounts to racial exclusion from the system of law.

The pattern of exclusion begins at the entrance gates to legal education and persists through employment practices and judicial appointments.

Law schools have relied too heavily on dubious test results, screening out black candidates whose personal attributes, grade averages, and strong commitment to a career in the law suggest that they should be admitted. It is no accident that—at every grade-point-average category—white applicants are more likely to be admitted to law school than blacks with the same grades.

As a result, the black law student population is only 4.5 percent of the total. But even that dismal figure tells only a small part of the story. The black share of law students has actually declined since 1976. Even as law schools increased minority enrollment, black enrollment stabilized. In 1971, blacks were about two-thirds of all minority law students; by 1981, they were barely half. Since 1971, the black share of law students barely moved—from 4 percent to 4.5 percent. But the Hispanic share doubled and the female share quadrupled.

After graduation, blacks are far less likely to go into private practice than whites. Less than three out of every 100 lawyers in the biggest and most prestigious firms are black. Over two-thirds of those firms have no black partners, and many employ no black lawyers at all. Few law schools have black professors.

Under the Reagan administration, the federal bench has been closed to blacks. Out of eighty-nine appointments to federal judgeships, only one was black. Whatever else we might say about President Carter, over 14 percent of his judicial appointments were black. And the Carter appointees won substantially the same ratings from the ABA [American Bar Association] as Mr. Reagan's appointees, so merit has nothing to do with it.

We have an obligation to ourselves, our profession, and to a democratic system based on the rule of law to eliminate the continued unequal access to the bar.

Law is said to be the second-oldest profession. Since the dawn of time, lawyers have told the rest of us what to do and how to do it. Now it is time for us to get our own house in order.

The problem is clear. Black citizens have been denied equal access to entry into the legal profession and equal access to all aspects of the profession.

The answer is also clear: affirmative recruitment and admissions policies and hiring policies consciously designed to remedy past and present exclusion.

Affirmative action has become a dirty word in Ronald Reagan's America. But it is an inescapable mechanism to redress past wrongs, to remedy present inequities, and to move a mean society to a posture of decency and fairness. We cannot allow affirmative action to become lost in a fog of legal technicalities and debate. Strip away all the endless and ultimately meaningless formulations of the problem, and we confront the essence of what affirmative action is all about. For in Lyndon Johnson's words:

> To be black in a white society is not to stand on level and equal ground. While the races may stand side by side, whites stand on history's mountain and blacks stand in history's hollow. Until we overcome unequal history, we cannot overcome unequal opportunity.

At issue is whether America's most powerful profession will include its largest minority. At issue is whether the prestige of the law can be maintained by a profession marked by racial exclusion. At issue is whether democracy's guardians will themselves be democratic.

I have faith that we will do so. I have faith that this great profession which—like America itself—has been about mobility and movement, about fulfilling aspirations, about providing tools that transcend circumstance, will finally do right and act right.

Justice Holmes said: "As life is action and passion, it is required of a man that he should share the passion and action of his time at the peril of being judged not to have lived."

I have faith you will share in the passion and action of our time, that you will do all in your power to democratize our profession, that you will personally plunge into the struggle to make the profession of law worthy of the principles inherent in our laws.

Our society has been moving backward over the past decade. We—each of us—have the clear responsibility to help move America forward again, to complete the unfinished Second Reconstruction and to defeat the selfish, greed-ridden counterrevolution that is debasing our national life.

Together, let us work to support a national leadership that understands the meaning of the words of Lord Brougham:

> It was the boast of Augustus that he found Rome of brick, and left it of marble; a praise not unworthy of a great prince. But how much nobler will be our Sovereign's

boast, when he shall have it to say, that he found law dear, and left it cheap; found it a sealed book—left it a living letter; found it the patrimony of the rich—left it the inheritance of the poor; found it the two-edged sword of craft and oppression—left it the staff of honesty and the shield of innocence!*

---

* Law Reform Speech of 1828 to the British Parliament.

A YEAR OF
CASCADING CHANGE

1989

My most pressing business concern in early January
1989 was fine-tuning a speech I was to give ten days
hence in Japan to Japan's most prestigious and powerful association of business executives, the Keidanren. My mission was
to set forth the concept of corporate social responsibility—
American-style—and help reaffirm the message they had
been hearing from many of their American counterparts:
that this was one means of reducing the tension—and out-
right hostility—that had increasingly come to characterize
American-Japanese relations.

Economic issues were at the heart of it. In the mid–1980s,
Japan had begun flexing its newfound economic might in
ways that startled and angered many Americans. No longer
was it just the matter of Japanese-made cars being widely
seen as a better product, and Japan's auto industry regarded
as more innovative and efficient. By the mid–1980s, Japanese
business prowess had also overwhelmed a good part of the

American electronics industry, from semiconductors to television sets. And while Japanese products streamed into the American market, to be eagerly purchased by American consumers, Japan's restrictions on foreign business activities in Japan and its protectionist trade policies rankled American companies and American politicians.

For all its growing tensions, however, the debate about Japanese business investment in the United States had largely been confined for most of the 1980s to the high-level arena of congressional hearings, meetings of governmental trade and diplomatic delegations and think-tank-sponsored discussions, and the opinion pages of the major newspapers. What transformed it late in the decade into a bitter public controversy was the juxtaposition of two things.

The first was the publication of several well-received books, such as Paul Kennedy's *The Rise and Fall of the Great Powers: Economic Change and Military Conflict from 1500 to 2000*, that discussed the newly powerful economic competition America faced from countries in Europe and Asia, including Japan. Those books declared that these countries' economic surge was substantially paring America's global economic hegemony, which had effectively been unchallenged since the end of World War II. Numerous conservative commentators and many ordinary Americans took umbrage at the notion that America's place in the world was "declining."

Second, the buying spree by Japanese businesses at the top of America's business and commercial real estate markets intensified the general economic anxiety. As the decade had deepened, several of America's most iconic companies, such as Firestone Tire and Rubber Company (which was bought by the Bridgestone Corporation of Japan in mid-1988), were figuratively sprouting a banner that read: Under new management.

The most stunning acquisitions were to come in late 1989. In October of that year, Japan's Sony Corporation bought the film studio Columbia Pictures Entertainment, Inc., for more than $3 billion. A few weeks later the giant Japanese development group Mitsubishi Estate Company bought a controlling stake in several prominent midtown Manhattan office buildings—including the landmark Rockefeller Center. The response of one New Yorker walking by Rockefeller Center when told of the deal by a reporter seemed to speak for many within and outside Gotham: "What?" the person said. "I don't believe you."

It became a cliché in some quarters in the United States for these deals to be described as an "invasion"—even though all of them had been sought by the American companies' executives and directors. In that regard, the charged word *invasion* and the attitudes behind it not only indicated that some Americans still thought of Japan in terms of the bitter war the two countries had fought in the South Pacific forty years earlier. It also reflected the fact that the controversy had an unmistakable racial facet to it. Many Japanese and some Americans asserted that Japanese investors were being unfairly criticized for having the skill and the resources to astutely apply standard capitalist practices to the American market. These observers noted that in actual dollar terms, British ownership of assets in America outstripped that of Japan, and Canadian and Dutch business investments were nearly as prominent. Yet those investments drew little notice and no hostility.

That flaring of the simmering controversy was eleven months away as I prepared in early January for my visit to Japan. My preparations were interrupted on January 6 when the news flashed that Hirohito, emperor since 1927, had died. His death was expected; he had been ill for some time with cancer. Nonetheless, given the admiration of him in Japan and the reverence the Japanese held for tradition, I wondered if the leaders of the Keidanren would ask me to postpone my trip.

They did not. I gave the speech on the day originally planned, advising my listeners in some detail about their need to expand the boundaries of their thinking concerning what constituted good business practices and what being a good corporate citizen meant to fit the American landscape. This advice included taking an active role in community improvement projects, supporting voluntary associations in the arts and education, and recognizing that the significant inclusion in their American workforce of blacks, other minorities, and women matters. Given that Japanese society placed great store in homogeneity and conformity, I especially wanted to impress upon them that they should understand and acknowledge in their practices the importance of America's great diversity.

I was focused on making sure my message got through to my Japanese hosts even as I conveyed my sympathies to them regarding the death of Emperor Hirohito. I had no inkling, beyond the inauguration of president-elect George H. W. Bush on January 20, of the seismic shift coming. Only later, in retrospect, did I fully comprehend that the seemingly innocuous act of the Keidanren leadership sticking to their schedule even in the immediate shadow of the emperor's death underscored what was to happen in 1989.

The year 1989 was the pivot point in moving the world from one era to the next. It was a year of cascading changes that introduced the world's nations and peoples to a new arrangement of global forces and relationships—the complex of issues and circumstances we are grappling with today.

Consider these crucial developments that occurred during those months:

The Soviet Union was listing badly from the failed ideology of communism. The economic and political reforms its charismatic and forward-thinking president, Mikhail S. Gorbachev, tried to implement would not be enough to prevent either the USSR's dissolution or Russia's eventual slide into a decade of widespread political and economic corruption at the top of its society and increasingly desperate social conditions for the Russian masses.

By 1989, the USSR's internal problems had produced a stunning spiraling impact throughout Europe, intensifying with lightning speed the "liberalization" and "democracy" movements in country after country of the old, tottering Warsaw Pact. By November 1989, the process of disintegration of the Iron Curtain, which had formed one ideological boundary of the forty-year cold war, was virtually complete. The Communist leaders of East Germany, their hold on power rapidly crumbling beneath them, opened the gates of its great symbol of modern political oppression, the Berlin Wall, as hundreds of thousands of East and West Berliners, who would soon live in a unified city, danced in the streets.

That kind of dancing would soon spread to the far end of another continent, Africa. For by then, it had also become clear that apartheid, South Africa's brutal system of racial oppression, once seen as being as deeply entrenched there as communism was in Eastern Europe, was swiftly collapsing, too. Three months later, in early February 1990, Nelson Mandela walked out of a prison near Cape Town, a free man for the first time in nearly thirty years. Amid a delirious worldwide celebration, Mandela began the negotiations that would bring the vote to black South Africans and majority rule to that country for the first time.

Some observers noted with wonder and hope that these two oppressive regimes met the same ironic fate. They had depended for their existence on the threat and application of brute force. But in the end their swift collapse occurred without violence, driven substantially by the power of words extolling the virtues of democracy. One American diplomat, a veteran of European cold war politics, told a reporter: "I guess history comes in waves, and this is one that is clearly cresting. It is not coups we are talking about. It is mass movements, people in the streets."

The spirit of liberation did not bloom everywhere, however. In June 1989, the Chinese government unleashed its
military against pro-democracy demonstrators in Beijing's
Tiananmen Square, where protestors had camped out since
April. The number who were killed—some put it in the
hundreds—has never been accurately established. And
soon, in the Balkans and in Rwanda, the dream of diverse
populations living among each other peacefully turned into a
nightmarish genocidal war. Those eruptions of savagery put
the world on notice that the capacity of human beings to do
great evil in the name of nationalism was undiminished—
and underscored all the more the imperative of using words
and speech for good.

KEIDANREN

Tokyo, Japan

January 11, 1989

*I*t is a great honor to be asked to address such a distinguished
group.* My topic is corporate social responsibility—a topic
about which much ink has been spilled, many words spoken, many
views aired. It is a topic that has profound implications for your
companies and for your business relations with the United States.

---

* The speech was titled "Corporate Social Responsibility—The American
Way."

It is also a topic I have some experience with. I spent over twelve years as president of two important American nonprofit institutions—the United Negro College Fund and the National Urban League. And much of my time in those posts was devoted to working closely with corporate leadership to define their social responsibility role and to help make it effective.

Today, as a lawyer with numerous corporate clients, and as a member of the board of directors of some of America's largest corporations, I find myself still involved in corporate social responsibility, but from the perspective of the corporation and its shareholders.

In that role, I have found that over the long term, the social responsibility function is every bit as important to a company's well-being as its financial or manufacturing or marketing functions.

Now, that might seem a gross overstatement. But just consider the experience of Johnson & Johnson, the pharmaceutical company. Johnson & Johnson had a strong reputation as a socially responsible corporation. It was deeply involved in community activities. It rebuilt its corporate headquarters in a downtown district at a time when it was fashionable for companies to leave the cities for suburban campuses. It was generous in support of charitable activities. And it had a hard-won reputation for integrity and fair dealing.

The Tylenol disaster hit. Poisoned capsules of the popular headache remedy were responsible for several deaths. We know now that some deranged person was responsible for the tragedy, but at the time it was suspected that the deaths were caused by lethal poisons introduced in the manufacturing process.

The fate of the entire corporation was literally at stake. But Johnson & Johnson immediately withdrew all Tylenol bottles from the marketplace—at tremendous cost. And it cooperated fully with the media and the authorities.

But the key factor that enabled the company to survive the disaster and to thrive afterward was its strong public image as a socially responsible company. People trusted Johnson & Johnson, and so they were willing to give it the benefit of the doubt—to keep buying the company's products and to demonstrate their faith that this company would not carelessly endanger its consumers and thus could not be held responsible for the tragedies.

In all the years preceding the Tylenol tragedies, no one at the company could have anticipated it, but it was their consistent dedication to socially responsible behavior which in the end proved to be their lifeboat. Successive managements implemented socially responsible policies because they felt it was part of the way a well-run company should operate. I'm sure they knew that there were benefits such as a good public image and a strong reputation. But who among those generations of socially responsible managers could have predicted that one day the company's fate would be decided by the public reputation it had earned?

Looking back, it is clear that is what happened. Another company would have gone under. But Johnson & Johnson not only survived, it was able to revive the Tylenol brand—something few people expected at the time.

Admittedly, that is an extreme case. Few companies are placed in such a perilous position, but it is also true that few companies can ignore the importance of establishing a reputation founded on socially responsible actions. Corporate social responsibility does impact on a company's bottom line, sometimes in very crucial ways.

My friend George Weisman, who was the CEO of Philip Morris, used to say that he was often asked how his company's contributions to arts and minority organizations helped the company. And he would answer that he knew those activities paid off in higher sales and in a better public image, but that he could not put a dollar figure on them. And then he said that his company also spent hundreds of millions of dollars in advertising—but he could not say with any precision how much that added to the bottom line, either.

So while it is not possible to quantify the bottom-line impact of corporate social responsibility, it is also not possible to do the same with other activities essential to the well-being of a business.

In the case of multinational corporations operating in the United States, the intangible benefits of corporate social responsibility take on an even greater dimension.

You know very well that the growing presence of foreign companies in the United States is a source of political controversy. You know that Japanese companies have been the most visible foreign investors for a number of reasons—the trade deficit, the sheer size and rapid growth of Japanese investments, the severe dislocations among American workers caused by foreign competition.

To effectively counter anti-Japanese sentiment, it is not enough for you to condemn "Japan-bashing" or to educate the public to the benefits of free trade and investment or even to negotiate more open markets.

Foreign-based multinationals must ensure that their American subsidiaries are seen by their workers, customers, and communities as operating in all important respects as American companies, equally committed to American corporate expectations.

That means, among other things, conforming to the highest standards of corporate social responsibility as defined by the practices and policies of leading American corporations such as IBM, Xerox, AT&T, and others.

Japanese firms have been extraordinarily successful in adapting to local market and labor-force conditions. To ensure your continued success, especially as you move manufacturing and other operations closer to their American markets, you must become as successful in adapting to local expectations of appropriate corporate social behavior.

At its most elementary level, that means abiding by the laws and, more importantly, by the spirit of the laws. I have no doubt that companies sophisticated enough to establish manufacturing and marketing organizations in the United States are also sophisticated enough to ensure that they comply with American legal requirements pertaining to financial integrity, government regulations, the environment, and other important aspects of business operations.

But because of the controversial nature of those investments, it is also essential for such companies to conform to the highest social-responsibility standards.

One of the great side benefits of the international marketplace is the greater familiarity with other cultures and other traditions we are all exposed to. I would urge you to become more familiar with American traditions of corporate social responsibility and to ensure that your American subsidiaries not only conform to those traditions but that they also assume leadership roles within their communities, just as they strive for leadership in technology, marketing, and other aspects of the business.

I believe the American concept of corporate social responsibility stems from the basic egalitarianism of American society. We never had a feudal period—never had lords and princes—never had an oligarchy. The American experience is rooted in the Enlightenment of the eighteenth century; in a revolution fought for liberty; in a national philosophy based on natural rights.

That is why, when America approached industrial maturity in the late nineteenth century, many of its leading businessmen voluntarily gave of their fortunes for the public good. Andrew Carnegie established free public libraries. Julius Rosenwald supported black education in the South. The Rockefellers, Fords, and others established foundations that donated money to worthy causes.

Some companies provided their workers with housing and health care. Others became involved in civic improvements. Over time, the business community became part of voluntary activities designed at improving the quality of life in the communities in which it operated and to help solve social problems on both a local and a national scale.

That long tradition came to maturity in the 1960s, when industry leaders looked out of their windows and saw flames rising in the riot-torn ghettos. They understood that their businesses rested on a foundation of social stability, and that unless they helped right social wrongs, their businesses could founder on the shifting sands of social instability.

Some of the more articulate business leaders began to talk of the social contract that binds corporations to the community. They openly stated that a corporate charter is a creature of the state, granted by the people, and can be withdrawn if the people conclude that the corporation is not acting in the public interest. They understood that the free enterprise system could only flourish if business met public expectations, that the old saying that much is demanded from those to whom much is given applied to corporations, too.

So the philosophy of corporate social responsibility, as it has evolved in America, is rooted in the belief that such behavior is an essential precondition for the continued existence of the free enterprise system. It was also recognized that in a free society, image is important—and that a good corporate image was both a defense against attacks on corporations and a policy supportive of business success.

Those beliefs were supported by surveys that showed that companies with strong social-responsibility programs enjoyed greater financial success than others. Put bluntly, in America, corporate social responsibility is good business.

What constitutes socially responsible behavior? I've already mentioned living up to the spirit of the laws. But that's a small part.

One important component is community involvement. An American company wields great power: It has resources, supplies jobs and tax revenues, and influences local communities in many ways. With that power must come responsible involvement.

America is a nation with a thriving voluntary sector. Important as government social welfare programs are, most of our lives are bound up in voluntary associations based in the community which focus on making our communities better places in which to live.

American companies are part of that nationwide phenomenon. They voluntarily beautify their neighborhoods, take an active role in community improvement projects, and are an important source of volunteer support.

John Bryan, the chief executive officer of Sara Lee Corporation, says he expects all of his executives to play a role in voluntary organizations, and part of their job assessment relates to that. His company has an office that places Sara Lee managers on the boards of voluntary organizations.

The largest national voluntary group in America is the United Way, which is based on business, labor, and individual involvement, with participation on both the local and the national levels.

Another aspect of corporate social responsibility is financial support of voluntary institutions. U.S. companies donate about $4.5 billion annually. They support colleges, hospitals, schools, arts and culture, social-welfare organizations, and a host of other worthy causes.

The amount companies give varies, but U.S. tax laws allow corporations to deduct up to 10 percent of pre-tax income donated to certified nonprofit organizations. The best companies usually target anywhere from 2 to 5 percent of their pre-tax income for such contributions, and often exceed that amount. In some communities, companies have formed "5-percent clubs" or "2-percent clubs," pledging to contribute at least that amount.

Since the 1960s, many corporations are focusing their giving more sharply—concentrating on supporting organizations actively working to solve social problems such as hunger, homelessness, and poverty and racism. They donate money, equipment, and volunteer support to those agencies. Some even run programs themselves, such as the American Express Company, which operates academies of finance in selected high schools.

Recently the National Urban League established a permanent endowment fund started with million-dollar donations from several large companies. Other voluntary agencies have benefited from corporate donations to make up for reduced government activities.

I should stress that much of this corporate activity is based on self-interest. U.S. corporations—and Japanese companies operating in the U.S.—face a growing labor-force crisis. White males—the traditional core of the labor force—are today a distinct minority of the workforce. Within the next few years, 85 percent of new entrants into the labor market will be women or minorities—the groups most often relegated to the margins and denied the experience, skills, and education required by today's economy.

That helps account for business leadership in efforts to improve the schools, for business support of programs aimed at improving black and minority education, and for business's concern with issues like poverty, housing, child care, and health, which impact on human potential and human resources.

That self-interest dimension is also behind the importance of corporate efforts to provide opportunities for blacks, women, and other minorities.

Today, half of all black children grow up poor. A third of all blacks are poor—that's triple the white rate. Social disorganization is sapping inner-city minority neighborhoods of their vitality and promise. Such conditions threaten business both in terms of having a future workforce that is capable of performing productively and in terms of the social stability upon which the free enterprise system depends.

While the issue of minority participation in the American economy should be an important concern for all U.S. companies, I believe it has a special meaning for subsidiaries of Japanese companies. The reason is the strained relations between Japan and the black community in the U.S.

We all know what has caused the strain—the unfortunate and derogatory remarks by leading figures in Japan, incidents such as the Sambo doll controversy, the expansion of trade relations with South Africa in the face of some American and European disinvestment.

More relevant, from the American black perspective, is the perception that Japanese-owned companies do not employ blacks and do not subcontract with minority suppliers, despite the importance of the $250-billion black consumer market to the success of many products made by Japanese companies.

Just last month, a study was released by the University of California at Berkeley that indicates Japanese automobile companies systematically avoid areas with large black populations in choosing U.S. plant sites.

The Congressional Black Caucus has launched a "buy American" campaign, there is growing talk of a boycott of Japanese goods, and there have been calls for congressional investigations to determine whether Japanese-owned companies are in violation of U.S. civil rights laws.

Thus, it will be necessary for Japanese companies to overcome those hostile relations by embracing policies that stress affirmative action, aggressive training programs for minorities, siting plants in inner cities or within reasonable travel time of such areas of black population, and building new relationships with the black business community by banking with minority-owned financial institutions and instituting strong programs of purchasing goods and services from minority-owned firms.

In doing that, it will be important to emulate the more successful American corporations and to work closely with established minority community-based organizations. Such programs will be doomed to fail if they are not implemented with the same research and determination that new business initiatives get.

There are new, emerging issues that impact on corporate social responsibility, as well. The growing importance of women in the workforce has led many employers to implement programs that encourage hiring and promoting of women and to establish day-care programs that enable parents to work. Recent studies show that such programs actually save companies money through fewer child-related work absences and lower employee turnover.

The aging of the workforce is another emerging issue that has led companies to address the special needs of their older workers in particular, and the aging, in general. Corporations are addressing health care, child care, and housing issues, too.

This is all part of the price of being a responsible corporate citizen in a society that values voluntary action and that insists on business being part of the solution to social problems.

Many people I've spoken with, including many Americans, tell me that the U.S. insistence on corporate social responsibility is alien to foreign companies, including Japanese companies. They say that it is an alien tradition and we cannot expect Japanese companies to understand it easily, much less to rush to corporate leadership in socially responsible ways.

But I would challenge that assumption. I believe it underestimates the Japanese capacity for adaptation, underestimates the universal human desire to do good and to be accepted as contributors to society's well-being, and underestimates the powerful elements in Japan's culture and Japanese business traditions that support the concept of social responsibility.

After all, it is to Japan that Americans have looked for leadership in employee relations. The old American tradition of top-down, authoritarian business operations is giving way to consensus management, thanks in large part to the example set by Japanese business.

So I would contend that corporate social responsibility is far from an alien concept to you. Although the American patterns are quite different, I see no reason why companies that have become the world's leaders in technology, production, and marketing cannot easily adapt to the American way in America. Indeed, American companies doing business in Japan have had to understand and adapt to Japanese traditions and expectations to be successful here.

Japan is a trading nation, and traders know the importance of conducting themselves in local markets in ways that conform to the expectations of their customers. Japan's prominent global economic position imposes even greater obligations. I believe that economic leadership implies greater moral responsibility and leadership. I believe that Japanese companies are not simply challenged today to emulate their American peers in responsible corporate behavior, but to excel and to lead.

For despite the stated philosophy of corporate social responsibility that is part of the American business tradition, and despite the outstanding records of many large and small companies, far too many U.S. firms have not lived up to their responsibilities.

Many American companies, even large ones, have been found guilty of illegal activities and of civil rights violations. Some have not been as supportive of community groups as they should. Others have avoided becoming involved in social progress.

Let me stress that they do not represent the norm. And let me also stress that they should not be your models. For as I see it, your role can be a creative one of leadership, of bringing American norms of responsible corporate action to new heights, of setting examples in corporate social responsibility as you have set them in manufacturing productivity.

The fact is that you do not have the luxury to avoid socially responsible activities or to slowly adapt to the lowest common denominator of U.S. practices.

The latent hostility to foreign-owned businesses and the protectionist cries make it urgent for Japanese companies to set new standards in corporate social responsibility, as they have in other aspects of business. Frankly, more will be expected of you. More will be demanded of you.

You can turn that to your advantage by moving swiftly to take the initiative and immediately set as a business priority the goal of becoming a leader in corporate social responsibility in the U.S.

I can think of no better investment in the long-term success of your American subsidiaries. I urge you to establish social responsibility committees on the boards and managements of your U.S. subsidiaries; to write business plans for social involvement; to implement minority hiring and promotion goals; to make excellence in social responsibility as important and as visible as excellence in quality and marketing.

And I urge this effort in your own corporate self-interest. Yes, there are moral considerations, social considerations, human considerations. But social responsibility is also a business consideration. Success in developing and implementing a social responsibility program can help ensure your corporate survival in the U.S., change the image of Japanese corporations as unconcerned about anything other than market share, and win new respect and customer loyalty in the world's largest consumer market. The famous American author, Herman Melville, once wrote:

> We cannot live for ourselves alone. Our lives are connected by a thousand invisible threads, and along those sympathetic fibers, our actions run as causes and return to us as results.

In your own self-interest, and in the interest of others, make your actions responsible actions. Make them actions that will return to you as good results. Recognize that responsible public policies are in your enlightened self-interest.

The world knows that the Japanese are a people who take duty and responsibility seriously. You are loyal and giving to your country, your government, your friends, and your families.

Consider your American employees, the local communities of your subsidiaries, and the people of the world as your family, too. They will support and care for you if you do the same for them.

A POWERFUL VOICE

Not Stilled, Still Heard

1993

The passing of Thurgood Marshall, whose casket rested before me in the great sanctuary of the Washington National Cathedral, was a sad contrast to the sense of revitalization, hope, and relief that just days earlier had attended the first inauguration of President Bill Clinton—the first Democratic administration in a dozen years, and one whose victory and progressive outlook stemmed from the social revolution Thurgood Marshall had played so central a role in forging.

Thurgood Marshall was a guardian of this nation's greatest treasure: He was a keeper of the flame of the American ideal. Both an advocate and a tribune of freedom, he appeared at a critical historical moment to help rescue from the dustbin of hypocrisy that glorious declaration of the Constitution: We hold these truths to be self-evident that all men are created equal and endowed by their creator with certain inalienable rights. The concept was so perfectly put—and so imperfectly realized until Charles Hamilton Houston, the great attorney and dean of Howard University Law School, began in the early 1930s to execute his grand strategy to destroy the legal bulwarks of segregation. A crucial element of that plan was the formation of a civil rights "brain trust." This diverse collection of brilliant attorneys—some black, some white—was spread throughout the country. Some had been waging such battles on an individual basis for years. Houston's great contribution was to provide a tactical, strategic, and intellectual coherence to the disparate efforts and, beginning in the early 1930s, to reinforce their thin ranks with numerous Howard Law graduates—such as Thurgood Marshall. He had excelled under Houston's relentlessly rigorous regime that had made Howard University Law School the West Point of black America's freedom struggle.

Marshall, graduating first in the Howard University Law School class of 1933, set the standard for all to follow. Howard Law was in fact Marshall's second choice for legal training. A Baltimore native, he had wanted to return home after graduating from Lincoln University, the historically black college in Pennsylvania, and enroll in the law school of the University of Maryland. But his application was rejected because he was black. Three years later, as a freshly minted law graduate, Marshall, working with Houston, successfully sued the University of Maryland Law School to admit a black Amherst College graduate, Donald Gaines Murray.

Tutored at Howard in both the utility and the majesty of the law as a force for justice, Thurgood Marshall used that knowledge, and his courage and commitment—and his wiles—to show America how to live up to its convictions. He cleared the brush, so to speak, that was blocking the nation's vision of and progress toward a more perfect, a more just, union.

Marshall did that by following the strategy Charles Hamilton Houston had devised: systematically challenging the legal bulwarks of racism in voting rights, housing, and, most of all, education—and by winning cases. His record as a Supreme Court practitioner was extraordinary. He won twenty-nine of the thirty-two cases he argued as the NAACP counsel before the Court. That superb Supreme Court record continued when President Johnson appointed him solicitor general of the United States in 1965. Representing the government, he won fourteen of the nineteen cases he argued, after which Johnson in June 1967 nominated him to the Court itself.

One can't overestimate the magnitude of Thurgood Marshall's achievement as an astute legal technician and tactician and as a persuasive advocate in the courtroom. He did battle with a legal system that until then had paid little heed to the exalted words of the Constitution. He and his fellow pioneers endured constant indignities in the courtrooms of the South—and the constant threat of physical harm outside the courts—as they tried case after case in places where the lives of black Americans, no matter how well educated, counted for virtually nothing.

But Marshall and his colleagues were also armed with something more than technical know-how and courage. They were armed with an understanding of the promise of America and the appeal of that promise to all Americans. And, finally, they were armed with a faith in the flexibility and adaptability of the Constitution—the faith that its words and the rhetoric of the American ideal had provided enough "give" in the American system to encompass black Americans' right to life, liberty, and the pursuit of happiness.

Thurgood Marshall believed in the Constitution of the United States. He believed that its words had a meaning beyond mere rhetoric; that if followed and applied properly, they offered America a way out of the "half slave, half free" paradigm it had followed since kidnapped Africans were first brought to Virginia's shores in 1619.

This was at first glance an extraordinary confidence to have in the moral capacity of white Americans during the 1930s, when antiblack bigotry seemed as pervasive and violent as in the early 1900s. But other astute observers of the racial scene also discerned momentous forces for change percolating beneath the society's white-supremacist surface. In the early 1940s, Gunnar Myrdal, the Swedish sociologist and author of the masterwork on race in America, *An American Dilemma*, expressed confidence that America could overcome its profound legalized bigotry. His optimism, he said, lay in the reality that America, unlike every other country in the West, had "a living system of expressed ideals for human cooperation which is unified, stable, and clearly formulated" and "that Americans, for all their differences, for all their warring and rivalries, were bound by a distinct 'American creed,' a common set of values that embodied such concepts as fair play and an equal chance for everyone." Nearly half a century later, Marshall would describe the Constitution to the journalist Carl Rowan, as "the greatest body of laws set out ever, and what to me, and to many people, is so extraordinary about it is that at this late date you find that it works."

At his death, one of Marshall's former law clerks, Yale Law School professor Paul Gewirtz, described Marshall as having "an heroic imagination." "He grew up in a ruthlessly discriminatory world," Professor Gewirtz went on. But he "had the capacity to imagine a radically different world, the imaginative capacity to believe that such a world was possible, the strength to sustain that image in the mind's eye and the heart's longing, and the courage and ability to make that imagined world real."

Thurgood Marshall's heroic imagination inspired me as a boy growing up in Georgia to dream of what was possible for my own future. In the late 1940s, I went with my father to an NAACP mass meeting and for the first time heard Marshall speak. His determination and confidence that blacks would gain their civil rights were so thrilling that I said to my father as we were walking from the church, "Daddy, I'm going to be a lawyer like Thurgood Marshall." My father said, "Okay, son." But he was looking at me as if I had lost my mind.

My father, however, missed part of the importance of Marshall, and of the men and women who were with him on the front lines of the struggle. They inspired by example. They not only gave black men and women, and boys and girls, the courage to face an often bitter present. They also gave them—gave me—the courage and the hope to dream that the future for black people could be gloriously different.

I never wavered in my determination to be a civil rights lawyer and to attend Howard University Law School. When I enrolled in September 1957, Marshall, then head of the NAACP Legal Defense and Educational Fund (LDF), gave one of the first major addresses of the school year. "This," he said, with tears in his eyes, "is Charlie Houston's Law School."

Marshall and the "Inc. Fund," as it was colloquially called, used the Law School's moot court room to rehearse arguments they would present in Supreme Court cases. These were informally formal sessions: Law professors from Howard and elsewhere, and other attorneys, sat as the judges and grilled the LDF presenters to expose weaknesses in their arguments. These were glorious moments for my classmates and me as we listened to the courtroom presentations of not only Marshall but such legal icons as Oliver Hill, Robert Carter, Constance Baker Motley, Jack Greenberg, William T. Coleman, and Robert Ming. During the breaks, we crowded around them, starry-eyed and seeing ourselves after law school following in their paths.

My sense of connection with Marshall and his work became more direct, though still distant, after I graduated. In

1960, while working as a law clerk for Donald L. Hollowell, the great civil rights attorney from Atlanta, I immediately became involved in the preparation for the lawsuit that led to Charlayne Hunter (now Charlayne Hunter-Gault) and Hamilton Holmes enrolling in the University of Georgia and ending its whites-only status. I didn't think that Marshall even knew my name. But, in 1961, during the NAACP annual convention that summer in Philadelphia, Ruby Hurley, the NAACP's regional field director for the Southeast and my supervisor, took me over to Marshall and began to introduce me. Marshall interrupted. "I know this boy, Ruby. He worked with Hollowell on the University of Georgia case."

His words made me stand a little taller at that moment, and, to my deep gratitude, his interest in me and support of me continued. In 1967, shortly after Marshall's appointment to the Supreme Court, I petitioned to practice before the Supreme Court. Wiley A. Branton, a lawyer for the Little Rock Nine and dean of the Howard University Law School, moved my admission to the Court. Branton also moved my admission to the Arkansas Supreme Court and I served as his deputy at the Voter Education Project of the Southern Regional Council. Branton was a former Inc. Fund lawyer and longtime friend of Marshall's. After the swearing in, I looked for a moment directly at Marshall and he, while keeping his face impassive, quickly but unmistakably winked his eye at me. My mother told me later that that gesture was like the laying on of hands.

Even so, although I was a disciple of Thurgood's, I never spent much one-on-one time with him. But we each felt a tacit bond that went very deep. This led to one of the signal honors of my life—being asked by his wonderful wife, Cissy, to give one of the eulogies at his funeral. It came as the direct result of Marshall's hearing me eulogize Wiley Branton, in the very same Washington National Cathedral in 1988. Thurgood and Cissy had sat in the second pew, amid a great host of civil rights veterans. After I had finished speaking, Cissy later told me, Thurgood turned to her and simply said, "Cissy, get Vernon."

WASHINGTON NATIONAL CATHEDRAL
Mount Saint Alban, Washington, D.C.
January 28, 1993

T he world is with us today, for the life and the teachings of Thurgood Marshall shine brightly all across the globe.*

People, in faraway places, many of whom may never have heard his name, aspire to live in the glow of the flame of liberty lit by Thurgood Marshall.

And people here in our nation breathe more freely because he lived among us, because he fought the good fight to secure their

---

* Eulogy at the funeral service for the Honorable Thurgood Marshall (1908–1993).

rights, because he used the lever of the law and the Constitution to propel his countrymen and women into a new era in which America came closer to its cherished ideals.

To those of my generation, growing up in the segregated South, Thurgood Marshall was more than a crusader for justice, more than a torchbearer of liberty, more than a wise and learned man of the law.

He was a teacher who taught us to believe in the shield of justice and the sword of truth; a role model whose career made us dream large dreams and work to secure them; an agent of change who transformed the way an entire generation thought of itself, of its place in our society, and of the law itself.

Picture, if you will, the inescapable power of the beacon light Thurgood Marshall beamed into our cramped and constricted community—a community in which the law ordained that we could only attend segregated, inferior schools; a community in which the law ordained that our parents be denied the right to vote; a community in which the law ordained segregation in the courtroom and exclusion of our parents from the jury box.

It was Thurgood's mission to turn these laws against themselves, to cleanse our tattered Constitution and our besmirched legal system of the filth of oppressive racism, to restore to all Americans a Constitution and a legal system newly alive to the requirements of justice.

By demonstrating that the law could be an instrument of liberation, he recruited a new generation of lawyers who had been brought up to think of the law as an instrument of oppression.

Those of us who grew up under the heel of Jim Crow were inspired to set our sights on the law as a career—to try to follow him on his journey of justice and equality.

So while all Americans are indebted to Thurgood Marshall's accomplishments, we who grew up in the sunlight of his deeds owe a special debt of gratitude.

We have heard much today about Thurgood Marshall's legal prowess, his extraordinary accomplishments, his burning devotion to justice, his influence on generations yet unborn.

But we must also acknowledge Thurgood Marshall, the family man. He truly loved his family—the source of his love, the focus of his love, the anchor in his life.

It is no accident that his sons, Thurgood and John, are involved in the law. Thurgood, Jr., is a lawyer who served as counsel to Senator Gore and Senate committees. He is currently a lawyer on Vice President Gore's staff. And John is a Virginia state trooper who led the Clinton–Gore motorcade from Monticello to Washington. His sons were his pride and joy. His love and admiration for Jean and Colleen, his daughters-in-law, were endless. His grandchildren, Melanie, Cecilia, and Thurgood William, turned this tough, no-nonsense justice of the Supreme Court into putty. He was always melting, giving in, and giving up when they visited him. Edward Patrick was born three weeks ago. Thurgood never saw him but flashed a wide smile when told of his birth.

Then there is the love for his dear wife, Cissy, who every day in every way for thirty-seven years, Thurgood was constantly, insistently, urgently saying to her, "Cissy, 'How do I love thee? Let me count the ways. I love thee to the depth and breadth and height my soul can reach, when feeling out of sight for the ends of being and ideal grace. I love thee with the breath, smiles, tears, of all my life! And, if God choose, I shall but love thee better after death.'"

We thank you, Thurgood, for your legacy of family and friendship, love and caring, crusading, and leading. Your voice is stilled, but your message lives.

Indeed, you have altered America irrevocably and forever.

Finally, as a lifelong Episcopalian, a former vestry man at St. Philip's in New York and a frequent congregant at St. Augustine's here in Washington—a man of faith—we hear you today in this National Cathedral reminding us of the biblical injunction: "Thou shalt love the lord thy God with all thy heart and with all thy soul and with all thy strength and with all thy mind and thy neighbor as thyself."

We hear you reminding us "to do justice, love mercy and to walk humbly with God."

And we hear you reminding us that the battle is not over, the victory not won, to be ever vigilant, to fight on until justice rolls down like water and righteousness a mighty stream.

In our sadness and distress, we hear you comforting and consoling us with the words of C. Austin Miles:

> I'm living on the mountain, underneath a cloudless sky,
> I'm drinking at the fountain that never shall run dry,

Oh yes! I'm feasting on the manna from a bountiful supply,
For I am dwelling in Beulah Land.

Farewell, Mr. Civil Rights—farewell, Mr. Justice Marshall—
we thank you for all you have done.

"Good night, sweet prince, and flights of angels sing thee to
thy rest."

ENTERING THE
THIRD MILLENNIUM

2001

I n the spring of 2001, I welcomed the invitation of my high
school basketball coach, T. Herman Graves, to speak at
the homecoming service of the First Congregational United
Church of Christ. Graves, now deceased, was a stalwart
member of First Congregational. After I finished high school,
he followed my career closely and we became friends. The
service was to take place on September 23.

By that Sunday, of course, America's, and the world's, future had been unalterably changed by the terrorist attacks on
the World Trade Center in New York and the Pentagon in
suburban Virginia less than a fortnight earlier. Ahead lay a
series of momentous decisions and dislocations that included
an invasion of Afghanistan in pursuit of Osama bin Laden,
the mastermind of the terrorist attacks; a wrongheaded and
calamitous invasion of Iraq, whose consequences will dam-
age American domestic and foreign affairs for years to come;
and the jettisoning of some of our cherished civil liberties,

an action whose effect is as yet unclear. In later years, London and Madrid, too, would suffer murderous attacks, as bin Laden's followers gave ample proof of the evil that motivated them. The order of the world we thought we understood had been literally blasted from beneath our feet. Three months later, Kofi Annan, the UN secretary-general, poetically and powerfully described the change in his acceptance speech upon receiving the Nobel Peace Prize in Oslo, Norway:

> We have entered the third millennium through a gate of fire. . . . If today, after the horror of 11 September, we see better, and we see further—we will realize that humanity is indivisible. New threats make no distinction between races, nations or regions. . . . in the early beginnings of the twenty-first century—a century already violently disabused of any hopes that progress towards global peace and prosperity is inevitable— this new reality can no longer be ignored. It must be confronted.

In the days and weeks after September 11, the shock of such a spectacular breach of the nation's defenses and the grief felt over the loss of thousands of innocents haunted Americans. In Manhattan, where I work four days a week, the sense of loss was even more palpable. Makeshift bulletin boards of pictures of people who had either worked at the World Trade Center or were thought to have been in the towers that day quickly appeared. They could be found in such well-traveled gathering places as Union Square Park and Grand Central Station and on such lonely outposts as the sides of stores and, even more poignantly, the front doors of brownstones and apartment buildings. That the people in the pictures were most often smiling made the likely answer to the desperate question penciled underneath—"Have you seen this person?"—all the more heartbreaking.

For a moment in those grief-stricken days, the desire for revenge threatened to overwhelm common sense and common decency. When it became known that the airplane hijackers were of Middle Eastern descent, the ugly specter of racial profiling was raised, which political and civic leaders at every level vigorously and rightly denounced. Intriguingly, in late September two surveys done by the Gallup Organization and Zogby International, respectively, discovered an unlikely source of support for the racial profiling of "Middle Eastern–looking" people as a defense against terrorists. Both surveys found that black Americans, who had always raised a justifiable hue and cry about police racial profiling against them, were more likely than other Americans to favor the racial profiling of Arab Americans and Arab nationals. The Gallup survey found that 71 percent of blacks supported requiring those of Arabic descent to undergo more intensive security checks at airports.

The findings stunned leading black politicians, scholars, and activists, who had criticized the racial profiling of Arab

Americans in unambiguous terms. But Harvard Medical School psychiatrist Alvin Poussaint, speaking to a *Boston Globe* reporter, said the findings indicated how shaken black Americans, whose deep-rooted patriotism is only rarely acknowledged, were by the attacks. Indeed, he said blacks may have found them all the more disorienting because their own long struggle in America had been rooted "in the turn-the-other-cheek, Christian principles of love, and Thou shalt not kill" and in reforming America through its political process.

Black support for racial profiling quickly subsided. Perhaps those favoring it in the heat of the moment later realized that given black Americans' varied physiognomies, it was ludicrous to think any racial profiling of those who "look" Arabic would be confined to those who actually were of Arabic descent. And the harassment and killing that occurred that fall of not only innocent Arab Americans, but also Sikhs—who are neither Arabic nor Muslim, but of Indian descent, and whose religion requires males to wear a beard and a turban—provided tragic evidence that many Americans have trouble telling the world's people of color apart.

Nonetheless, the two polls' findings did prove a point, namely, that those who favor racial profiling always suggest it be applied against some other group of people, not their own.

Fortunately, the tragedy of September 11 had provoked exalted sentiments as well—an extraordinary cascade of patriotic feeling and a spirit of national unity that went far deeper than the American flags and flag decals that quickly sprouted from doorways and windows of homes and office buildings, and from the bumpers and radio antennas of cars and trucks. The loss of multitudes of innocent people, transformed by their brief biographies in the media from faceless victims to colleagues, neighbors, and friends, and the widely reported acts of kindness and heroism that occurred that day impressed upon millions that one way to oppose terrorism was to love thy neighbor, to value decency and our common humanity.

An October survey by the National Opinion Research Center of the University of Chicago provided the statistical evidence for what was apparent. It found that Americans' pride in their country, and their confidence in the country's leadership—not only the office of the presidency (and President George W. Bush himself) and the Congress but also in such sectors as organized religion and financial institutions— had increased by double-digit margins. So, too, had Americans' faith in their fellow citizens: Two-thirds of those polled said they believed that most people are helpful, a gain of 21 percentage points over the response to that question a year earlier. The director of the survey said its findings reflected "a fundamentally new state of mind of the American people."

It was those three realities of our new world—that the attacks of September 11 had pushed us into the third millennium through a gate of fire; that we were forced to consider such massive change with a fundamentally new outlook; and that kindness and decency still remain powerful antidotes to hatred and violence— that became the foundation for my speech at the First Congregational Church that day.

First Congregational Church, United Church of Christ
Atlanta, Georgia
September 23, 2001

*T*hank you for inviting me here today and for this opportunity to join you for your homecoming service.

This is also a homecoming for me—returning again to my hometown of Atlanta, to the welcoming arms of the black church—to reaffirm the values I learned here as a youngster, values that have guided my life.

For what I am and what I have achieved, I owe to that experience and to the people who guided me while I have run this race— through all of life's trials and tribulations, joys and triumphs.

I had planned to talk about those people today—about my parents who steered me on a straight and narrow path, about my teachers at Walker Street, E. A. Ware, and David T. Howard high schools, the counselors at the Butler Street YMCA, and about the role of the black church, and its historic mission as a beacon of hope and opportunity for black people.

Such a talk would have been appropriate for your homecoming theme of "for the glory of God and the good of humankind."

And it would have been fitting for me, whose fond memories of those loving, caring individuals and institutions grows stronger with every passing year.

But like all Americans, my thoughts this past fortnight have been elsewhere.

My thoughts have been with those many thousands of innocent victims of horror, with their families and friends, and with our wounded nation.

My thoughts have been about how we got to this perilous situation, what we must do to overcome it, and of the need to affirm our values—especially as those values come under attack from the forces of evil.

The world has changed radically in the past decade. It is a world that has become more complex and more integrated than ever.

Technology has changed our economy and our lives. We have instant communications across the globe—what once took days and even weeks now takes seconds. CNN's cameras sent pictures of the Trade Center and the Pentagon disaster around the world as it was happening.

The great worldwide division of the past half century was the struggle between communism and freedom. Freedom won. The American model of freedom and free markets is now the world's model.

But freedom's victory is being tested in a world of diverse cultural, social, and economic traditions. The giant leap forward of technology and free trade have left many behind. The pervasive march of modernity disrupts traditional cultures. Worldwide migrations sharpen culture clashes. The industrial world ages while the developing world's population growth strains its ability to feed or employ its people. The power of new multinational institutions—the European Union, the World Trade Organization, worldwide corporations, and mass media, among others—breeds resentment and distrust.

About the only constant is the craving for full participation in political decisions that affect people's lives and in the economic decisions that affect their livelihoods.

That is why many people believe the rush for markets and profits leads to exploitation, unemployment, and human suffering. Americans, who have benefited from the triumph of markets, dismiss such feelings at our peril. For our vision of a fair, democratic capitalist society must include social justice and equitable division of the benefits of the free market.

Absent that, there is a tendency toward a turning within, a rejection of the outside world and modern ways, a rush to a form of traditionalism that wallows in envy and hate—a traditionalism that is not only economically counterproductive but reflects insularity and deep mistrust of all outsiders.

Diversity within unity is a sign of a robust culture. But withdrawal to hate and despair is a sign that evil is taking root. It betrays those who should be helped to participate in this new world, not encouraged to tear down their only real hope for progress.

Broadening the base of freedom and prosperity should be a cornerstone of America's policy. Not only because it might shrink the numbers of disaffected who can be recruited for terrorism. But because it is the right thing to do, the just thing, the moral thing. And it is also practical, for the more people who are productive and well fed and housed, the higher everyone's living standards will be—the world over.

But it is easy for many of us to be so fixed upon existing poverty and injustices that we confuse cause and effect. They are not the causes of terrorism.

A hatred of modernity and a love of evil are the causes of terrorism. And in this world, as we have so painfully seen, there is no hiding place from terrorism.

It is good to remember *that* at a homecoming service whose theme is "for the glory of God and *the good of humankind*." For destroying innocent lives has nothing to do with the good of humankind and everything to do with pure, unadulterated evil.

Evil has always been with us. Black people have experienced more of it than most. But the deeds of that day of infamy, September 11, were perpetrated by malevolent people who willfully murdered thousands of innocent people. In the words of Isaiah:

> Their feet run to evil, and they
> Make haste to shed innocent blood;
> Their thoughts are thoughts of iniquity;
> Wasting and destruction are in their paths.

Our response to the evil of September 11 is very clear. By definition, those acts were acts of war. By the principles of international law, self-defense, and common sense, we will strike back at the networks of terrorists who attacked us, the networks that support them and are committed to harm us, and the governments that give them shelter, arms, and resources.

War is a terrible thing. No one in his or her right mind wants it. But if it is forced upon us—as it has been—it must be pursued as Jeremiah says, with "fury like fire, and burn that none can quench it, because of the evil of your doings."

Even as we do so, we must be clear about what we are fighting for and why. For many Americans today, gripped by shock and trauma, simple revenge is enough. But great causes cannot be rooted in negativism. Nor can they be driven by raw emotions.

We did not go into World War II solely to avenge Pearl Harbor or because the Nazis were bad. We went to war—and won that war—to defend freedom and democracy from those who would replace it with tyranny and despotism.

Yes, our democracy was flawed. But our affirmation of democracy during World War II set the stage for its expansion and growth in the postwar era.

Now we are called upon to defend freedom from chaos and mindless terror. This new kind of war will be long and difficult, for the enemy is elusive and as we have seen, modern societies are highly vulnerable.

We will win that war if we fight *for* our American values and if we act consistent with those values.

We pride ourselves on being an open, free society. That is what the terrorists hate about us. They want a closed, controlled society.

If we defeat them militarily but in the process become less free, less open—they will have won.

Obviously, we now will face restrictions that try our patience. Tightened security in public places, bag checks at buildings and airports, and all the delays and petty annoyances of necessary precautions.

Such measures are part of being at war, and they are acceptable limitations so long as our basic freedoms are intact.

We must not allow the inroads on those basic freedoms that can happen in times of national emergency. In World War I, there was a "red scare" in which the government ignored constitutional rights like freedom of speech. In World War II, Japanese Americans, including U.S. citizens, were forced into detention camps.

Such things happen during wartime, when feelings run high. They must not happen again. For even if we win the battles, we would lose the war. We must be on guard against subverting our Constitution and our civil liberties in the name of defending the Constitution and liberty.

The attack itself has been portrayed by many as an attack on capitalism, an attack on America's military power, an attack on globalism, even an attack on America's role in the Middle East.

It may be all of those, but only in part. The central target of that attack was America's values—as an open, democratic, multicultural society.

The terrorists who turned civilian planes into destructive missiles were sending a message. It was a message that was not addressed to the White House or the Pentagon or to Wall Street. It was addressed "To whom it may concern," and that means all Americans and all free people.

On the morning of September 11, I was in New York—working in my office on the sixty-second floor at 30 Rockefeller Plaza. My secretary was on the phone with my wife, looking out the window, and saw the first plane hit the first tower. She called out— and together we stood horrified and watched the second plane slam into the south tower of the World Trade Center.

I spent the rest of the day the same way many of you did— watching the televised reports of the disasters for hours on end. Like you, I have seen interviews with the survivors, the lucky ones who escaped the burning towers in time. I have walked the streets where, on every corner, are sad, homemade posters with names and pictures of the missing, pleading for information about them.

Those survivors and the victims on the posters are whites and blacks, Asians, Latinos, and Arabs. They are Christians, Jews, and Muslims. They are executives and janitors, bureaucrats and messengers. They are rich and they are poor. They are young, old, and middle-aged. They are Republicans and Democrats. Politically, some are on the far right, some are on the far left, and some may even have sympathized with some of the terrorists' ideas.

But they are all Americans. And in the eyes of the terrorists, they all stand for values that are central to the American fabric. And that was enough to make them targets, just as you and I and all our loved ones are targets now.

Black Americans hold America's values dearly. At times, it seemed as if we were the only ones who did. When this nation was in the grip of racism and segregation, it was black people who reminded America of its basic values of freedom and democracy. It was black Americans who helped America to close the gap between its beliefs and its practices.

Now that America is warring on terrorism, it is black people who can remind America that we know it well. For we remember the terrorism that swept the South during the civil rights movement and the lynchings before that. We remember the four little girls killed in the bombing of a Birmingham church. We know that dangerous rhetoric can lead to acts of lunacy that kill innocents. And we know that the surest defense against terrorism is affirmation of America's basic values—the values we have learned in our churches, the values we have fought and died for.

I cannot speak of our values without invoking the role of the black church in our lives. For the church is our preeminent institution. It has been a prime instrument in our quest for social justice. It has been the vehicle that brought us forward and gave us the tools and principles to make our way in a hostile environment.

That has been and continues to be the historic role of the black church. It was led by black preachers, often unlettered, untutored working people, who helped break the chains of slavery and oppression, and mobilized us to win the struggle for civil rights.

That history has a lesson for all Americans in this time of trial. For it demonstrates that military might must be accompanied by moral force, that arms raised in righteousness are more powerful than arms raised in anger, that the coming struggle must reinforce our values, not weaken them.

All Americans, as they bear the heavy load of this struggle, must listen to the words of James Cleveland:*

> I've come too far from where I started from. Nobody told me the road would be easy. I don't believe he brought me this far to leave me.

It was the black church that gave us the spiritual strength to battle our way to equal rights. It was the black church that gave the civil rights movement many of its leaders and its troops in the revolution for equality. It was the fervor of the black church that helped us to remind ourselves and the nation that this land, America, is ours, too.

And America has responded to our pleas and our demands by changing. Not as fast as we might wish. Not as willingly as we hoped. But change it has. We must understand that change and help move it further. For we cannot be frozen in a bitter past; we cannot forever lick yesterday's wounds.

We must recognize that—thanks to the civil rights movement— America in the second half of the twentieth century underwent a revolution as deep and as strong as those we read about in school. It was a revolution as defiant as the Boston Tea Party, as basic as the agricultural revolution, as important as the Industrial Revolution, and as smart as the information age revolution.

---

* The Reverend Dr. James Cleveland (1931–1991) was a celebrated minister, as well as a producer and performer of gospel music.

It was a revolution that saved America's soul, a revolution that put legal segregation in the dumpster, a revolution that turned America inside out and upside down.

We changed America with our brains, blood, sweat, tears, tired feet, and beat-up heads. Too many paid the ultimate price of death.

And if we have done so much when we had so little, think how much more we can do now that we have so much more.

And there is much unfinished work to do, for we cannot allow how far we have come blind us to how far we have left to go.

So we must rise to the challenge of doing more—and doing it better. We must find creative new ways to tackle old, intransigent problems. We must take as our credo, these words of William James:

> What we do, compared to what we can do, is like comparing the waves on top of the ocean with the ocean's mighty depths.

That was the kind of thinking that inspired the civil rights movement when we plunged into the depths to pluck out the buried treasures of our precious rights and opportunities.

We have in fact changed the face of America and the world. We are a great people, and we are patriotic Americans. Take heart from our glorious past and be encouraged by it because it can inspire us to understand the great things we can do when we come together to do them.

Now, as we and our fellow Americans face the dangers and snares of a new war against the evils of terrorism, we once again turn to the faith and values of our church, and we say, with the Psalmist:

God is our refuge and strength, a very present help in time of trouble, therefore we will not fear, though the earth be removed, and though the mountains be carried into the midst of the sea.

That, members of historic First Congregational Church, is your charge to keep, your calling to fulfill, your rendezvous with destiny. To that end, may you neither stumble nor falter. Rather, may you mount up with wings as eagles. May you run and not be weary. May you walk together, children, and not be faint.

A TRUE ALFALFAN AT HEART

2004

If it's a truism that politics is the practice of war by other means, organizations like Washington's Alfalfa Club are as necessary to the conduct of the nation's affairs as political parties. For they are places where the combatants from all sides can find a momentary respite from the battlefield, and also find that on a personal basis they can be friends. The club was founded in 1913 by four officials from the Department of Agriculture, and its purpose was "merely to make life brighter and more comfortable for its members." That is still the case; but fortunately in the decades after the 1960s, its members came to recognize that women, black Americans, and other people of color also met the broad qualification of having achieved distinction in politics, public service, and other sectors of American life. I was elected to membership in the Alfalfa Club in 1989 and served a term as its president from 2003 to 2004. My predecessor was Senator Thad Cochran of Mississippi; and my successor was Senator John McCain—following the club rule that the presidency be rotated annually between Democrats and Republicans. The central purpose of the Alfalfa Club is not just to enable some members of the high and mighty to rub elbows with other members of the high and mighty. It is also to use humor to ease the extraordinary tensions of the politics practiced in a place that is not only the capital of the United States but still the most important political capital in the world.

The pressures of the political arena there are enormous, and often wrenching, on a daily basis. Elected and appointed officials must juggle the interests of multiple constituencies that often stand in sharp opposition to one another, navigate the increasing complexity of fund-raising and lobbying, and joust with each other over proposed legislation and rules that are scrutinized by the media. The advent of instantaneous mass communications and the twenty-four-hour news cycle has served to increase that pressure to a constant fever pitch.

The Alfalfa dinners, however, offer a reminder that individuals can be members of opposing political forces on this or that issue and yet still be part of a broader community. The mechanism for that is humor—sharp sometimes, but always fundamentally good-natured. And precisely because the competition out in the public arena can be so fierce, the humor at Alfalfa Club dinners has to be not just good but top-notch. The audiences are so powerful and the stakes for embarrassment so high that if you are to be one of the speakers, you'd have to be a fool not to get professional help. And you would have to be an even bigger fool if you didn't hire a writer the caliber of Landon Parvin, of Fredericksburg, Virginia, to help you with your remarks and your rehearsals.

Over the years, Landon and I developed a partnership and a friendship. We are an odd couple—a tall, black Democrat and a short, white Republican. But it works because we genuinely like each other and trust each other—and that is the basis of the best kind of relationship between speaker and writer. It's a good model for politicians in general, as well.

NINETY-FIRST ANNUAL DINNER
OF THE ALFALFA CLUB
Hilton Hotel, Washington, D.C.
January 24, 2004

*T*hank you, Alfalfans and guests.

Mr. President, I feel like I'm at one of your cabinet meetings—a blind man in a room full of deaf people.

We were worried that a number of Alfalfans who work on Wall Street and in the mutual fund industry might not make it tonight, but fortunately due to a hole in the prosecution's case, we're all here.

Before I hand over my presidency to my successor, let me take a moment, regardless of whether we are Christian, Jew, or Muslim, and thank the Almighty, the one who controls our destiny as a nation—Karl Rove.

Thank you, Karl,

As usual, this is a stellar turnout of power, wealth, and celebrity—billionaires, Supreme Court justices, cabinet secretaries. I understand that former treasury secretary Paul O'Neill is not dining with us tonight. At the pleasure of the White House, he is dining at Guantanamo.

As I look around this room, I am reminded that it's a long, long way from the public housing projects of Atlanta to the presidency of the Alfalfa. I only wish my daddy—Strom Thurmond—could see me tonight.

Over the last year, I have received many kudos for my leadership of this club—true, most of them from me—but I have tried to expand the diversity of the Alfalfa Club, by reaching out to rich people of *all* colors and creeds.

But I have one last remaining duty—to introduce my successor.

Four years ago tonight, John McCain was in the snows of New Hampshire proclaiming that he would be president—John, *your dream has come true.*

John, as you know, once served as a navy pilot on an aircraft carrier. First, the president beats him for the nomination, then he steals his suit.

John McCain is a man who believes in duty, honor, country. As a POW, he refused release unless the Vietnamese also released his fellow prisoners. What honor, what strength, what moral courage! What the hell is such a man doing as president of this Club?

But, my fellow Alfalfans, I want to pay tribute to John. He is a man who spent years being tortured by tormentors trying to break his spirit. But John stood up to Trent Lott and Tom DeLay.

And he is here tonight.

Ladies and gentlemen, Alfalfa's new president, Senator John McCain.

PRAISING THE LORD
AND THE LEGACY

2008

One of the great joys of my years at the Howard University Law School was worshipping at the Andrew Rankin Memorial Chapel. During the past decade, I've been honored each spring by the invitation of Dean Bernard L. Richardson to speak at the Chapel service. I was especially grateful in the spring of 2008, amid the controversy surrounding Senator Barack Obama's former pastor, Reverend Jeremiah Wright, to return to its pulpit. I felt compelled, given the harsh generalizations it provoked in the media about the black church, to share my thoughts on an institution I've known and been closely involved with all my life. I also wanted to publicly acknowledge my debt to five great black preachers who have greatly influenced my life— William Holmes Borders, Martin Luther King, Jr., Benjamin E. Mays, Howard Thurman, and Gardner C. Taylor. The path their eloquence, courage, and conviction inspired me to pursue represents in some significant ways the magnificent journey black Americans forged from the 1930s to the present. As a child I was fortunate to see fully the strengths of black America—its individual heroic figures and its ordinary men and women, many of whom lived lives of quiet heroism; its communal cohesion; and its unshakeable determination to secure civil rights and equal opportunity. I was privileged to grow up during an era when black Americans, and their allies among other Americans, taught America's government and its white majority that the words of the Constitution truly meant that America was to be a democracy—no exceptions.

The bedrock of that extraordinary movement was the black church and its steadfast commitment to faith in the power of the Lord and the power of faith itself.

This book began with my childhood grounding in the black church tradition, a tradition in which speaking publicly about issues of the larger society played an important role. It ends with my speaking from the pulpit of a historic black church in large measure about a presidential primary contest few would have dared envision: a black man and a white woman as the two leading candidates to capture their party's presidential nomination. For all of the work left to be done along the color line, the mere fact that such a contest has occurred reaffirms blacks' long-held faith that America's potential to realize a more perfect union remains substantial.

In one sense, however, there was no little irony buried in my celebration of the rise of both Hillary Clinton and Barack Obama, for they were the central figures in two of the three instances when my political instincts have been absolutely wrong—and all have involved aspirants for the presidency.

In 1973, I suggested to Jimmy Carter that he should give up his ambition to be president. I was wrong—as he reminded me two days after his election in 1976. When First Lady Hillary Clinton sought my counsel about running for the U.S. Senate from New York, I was wrong again, suggesting to her that that was not a good idea. She ran, of course, and won by a substantial margin. Later, at a birthday party for President Clinton on Martha's Vineyard, I publicly pleaded guilty to being wrong and apologized to Senator Clinton. I was wrong a third time in a dinner conversation with Barack Obama in my kitchen in November of 2006. Obama and I had met in Chicago when he was an unknown Illinois Senator, at a lunch convened by John Bryan, former chairman of the Sara Lee Corporation. As a result of that lunch, my wife, Ann, and I hosted a highly successful fundraiser in Washington for Obama's candidacy for the U.S. Senate.

In November I suggested to him that the 2008 presidential election was not his time. How wrong I was. I also told him that if he did, in fact, run, I would support Hillary Clinton, who had been my friend since 1969. But I promised him that if he ran and was successful, I would enthusiastically back his candidacy for president of the United States. Obama didn't respond in any verbal way; he merely nodded his acceptance of my position.

My being wrong did not disqualify me from standing before the congregation in Andrew Rankin Memorial Chapel
and trying to put the momentous 2008 presidential campaign
in its proper historical context—one in which the influence
of the black church flows like a deep, mighty stream "inspiring a thirst for social justice [and] igniting the spirit of activism to secure a more just, more equal society." My purpose
in doing so was not to take sides in the historic fight, but to
acknowledge the wonder and gravity of the moment and the
journey of all three candidates in the race at that time—
Hillary Clinton, Barack Obama, and John McCain. I sought
to follow my friend Bill Safire's definition of a speech's most
exalted purpose—"to inspire, to ennoble, to instruct, to rally,
to lead."

ANDREW RANKIN MEMORIAL CHAPEL,
HOWARD UNIVERSITY
Washington, D.C.
April 27, 2008

*D*r. Crawford, Dr. Richardson, pulpit guests, the choir, my
sisters at Delta Sigma Theta, my brothers in Omega Psi
Phi, students, alumni, friends, faculty of Howard University:
    Once again, Dean Richardson has summoned me to this
hallowed pulpit, on this historic campus, the capstone of black
higher education. I first worshipped in Rankin Chapel fifty-

one years ago as a first-year student here at the Howard University Law School. Mordecai Johnson was president and Dean Daniel Hill stood where Dean Richardson now stands at Rankin.

This is a stark reminder that I am now a senior citizen—as set forth by a friend, Henry Lewin, now deceased, who in his holiday letter of 2007 reminded me that I was "born before television, before penicillin, before polio shots, frozen foods, Xerox, plastic, contact lenses, Frisbees, and the pill. Born before radar, credit cards, split atoms, laser beams, and ballpoint pens. Born before pantyhose, dishwashers, clothes dryers, electric blankets, air conditioners, and drip-dry clothes."

I am so senior that I got married first, *then* lived together. In my time, having a meaningful relationship meant getting along well with my cousins. So senior that I was "born before house husbands, gay rights, dual careers, and computer marriages. Before day-care centers, group therapy, and nursing homes."

But there is one thing that transcends the ages—from the very first time of the very first black church, where the doors swung back on welcome hinges and black people entered the sanctuary feeling and singing, as I hope you are feeling this morning at Rankin:

There's a sweet, sweet spirit in this place,
And I know that it's the Spirit of the Lord,
There are sweet expressions on each face,
And I know they feel the presence of the Lord.

The black church has helped define who I am and what I believe. The black church has sustained me in dark midnights, lifted my spirits, and inspired me to make every round go higher and higher.

That is the calling and legacy of the black church and its great preachers who shepherd its flocks.

The black church has been the place for the sustenance of our souls—the place that mobilized us to fight for justice and the place that taught us the rules of righteous living, the moral principles that allow us to stand tall and proud, to do right, to act right, to think right.

Throughout our history, the black church and our black preachers have been like a mighty river coursing through rocky mountains and verdant valleys, existing on many levels and fertilizing black thought and black life.

To me, the legacy of the black church is inseparable from its eminent preachers. Black preaching is many things—an exalted art form, whose foremost practitioners hold a place among the best of singers and artists and musicians. Those black preachers are virtuosos of the spoken word, masters of verbal nuances and rhythms that touch the soul.

Black preaching is a spiritual endeavor, whose greatest exemplars unite their flock with God and shine a brilliant light into the dark corners of the soul.

Historically, the black church has been a unifying force, uniting people behind ancient truths and contemporary struggles.

The black church has traditionally been a change agent—inspiring a thirst for social justice, igniting the spirit of activism to secure a more just, more equal society.

It was black preachers, unlettered, untutored working people, who helped break the chains of slavery and oppression. It was black preachers who helped mobilize us to win the struggle for civil rights.

It was the eloquence and unrelenting passion for liberty by black preachers that helped America look deeply into its own soul to recognize that awful gap between what is and what ought to be; between the dictates of the Constitution and the reality of Jim Crow; between the bright promise of democracy and the ugly fact of segregation.

The preaching, the prayers, and the songs of the black church strengthened the resolve of the poorest among us to be free, to walk with dignity, to act with courage.

That exalted tradition has left its mark on you and me.

I have heard country preachers in one-room, back-road churches ministering to the black poor, and I have heard preachers in the world's most prestigious cathedrals exhorting presidents and kings.

But of those many preachers I have heard, five have left an indelible mark on me.

The first was William Holmes Borders, Sr. I shall never forget his sermon in August 1948, right after the national political conventions nominated their presidential candidates. I was thirteen years old and had listened to those conventions on the radio with my father. The following Sunday at Wheat Street Baptist Church in Atlanta I heard Reverend Borders, resplendent in his white double-breasted suit, preach a sermon titled, "Planks in God's Platform."

He spoke of love, faith, hope, and charity, and then he reared back and said, "For my party, I nominate a man who was born in a manger, who split time into B.C. and A.D.," and he went on to proclaim Jesus as his candidate.

The Democrats nominated Truman. The Republicans nominated Dewey. Borders nominated Jesus.

He made religious truths relevant to current political realities.

The second preacher who left his mark on me, and undoubtedly you, was Martin Luther King, Jr., I can still hear his address to the Atlanta NAACP Emancipation Proclamation program on January 1, 1956. This young preacher speaking in his hometown electrified big Bethel Church with the moral, ethical, and religious dimensions of the Montgomery Bus Boycott.

When Martin concluded his thundering oration, my aspiration to be a soldier in the civil rights army was reaffirmed, my commitment to service irrevocable. I was privileged to work with him and the SCLC in voter registration and citizenship education programs throughout the South.

A third preacher who influenced me was Benjamin E. Mays, the beloved president of Morehouse College.

In the early sixties, Dr. Mays called my law office. First, a call from Benjamin Elijah Mays was like a call from God. He wanted me to substitute for him in Buffalo, New York. I couldn't believe what I was hearing. I asked him how he could ask me to take his place when he'd never heard me speak and I did not attend Morehouse. Dr. Mays said he had heard me six months earlier at chapel. "But you weren't there," I said.

And Dr. Mays said, "Yes, I was. I came late and sat in the balcony. You go to Buffalo; you'll do fine."

Then he said something that has stayed with me all my life, and I pass it on to you—"Son, whenever you're speaking always do your best because you never know who's listening. Remember that."

The fourth preacher in my experience was Dr. Howard Thurman, who taught here. He was insightful, mystic, a philosopher and theologian. When I was gravely wounded in 1980, Dr. Thurman shared his taped sermons and meditations.

The day before ending my ninety-nine-day stay in the hospital, I called him to say the doctors released me. He said, "Well, God's going to be mighty relieved." "Why is God going to be mighty relieved?" I asked. He answered, "Because he's tired of hearing me talk about you three times a day."

I was blessed to be included in that small group of civil rights leaders who individually journeyed to Dr. Thurman's home in San Francisco for three-hour sessions. There he counseled about matters personal, political, and spiritual. And he was always there with his pastoral counseling and intellectual guidance.

The fifth of these magnificent preachers—and one who occupies a very special place in my heart—is Gardner Calvin Taylor.

Gardner C. Taylor is perhaps our greatest preacher, the poet laureate of the pulpit, the bringer of passion and eloquence that stirs the heart and stimulates the mind. Gardner Taylor lights fires with his preaching—fires sparked by the power of his words and the force of his logic.

Let me add one note because it has—and always will have—great meaning for me. I was an unwilling participant in a well-publicized legal process in Washington not so long ago. Five times I went to testify before the grand jury and once to testify before the U.S. Senate in impeachment proceedings.

Each night before I was scheduled to testify, Gardner Taylor was on the phone, calling to pray with me.

Gardner Taylor would speak to the Lord, telling him what to do. I can still hear Gardner's voice saying, "Lord, tomorrow morning Vernon has to go into the grand jury room, and I want you to go with him and stand by him and prop him up on every weak and leaning side."

That meant everything to me—my friend Gardner pleading with the Lord to wrap his long arms of protection around me. His powerful, personal faith was, and is, for me like the tree planteth by the rivers of water—strong, immovable, sturdy, unshakeable.

Now, these five very different great preachers—all of whom have preached here in Rankin Chapel—had different styles and strengths, but they all shared a zeal for social justice—and a passion for responsible behavior. They were disturbers of the unjust peace.

Those attributes have always been at the core of the black church's teachings, at its best, and they instruct us to aspire to do things far beyond what we thought were the limits of our possibilities.

That age-old mission is why the black church cannot be defined in narrow terms. The black church's contributions and value cannot be descriptively or ideologically confined to the use of sixty-second sound bites clipped out of a full sermon of any black preacher in any church on any given Sunday.

The black church can no more be defined by one or two phrases spoken within a full sermon by Jeremiah Wright than the white church can be defined by Pat Robertson's assertion that 9/11 was a manifestation of the wrath of God.

Part of the beauty of Rankin Chapel, and what constitutes its mission and value, is that it has taken the opposite approach.

Rankin has not succumbed to parochialism.

On the contrary, Rankin presents a rich selection of the tapestry of the black church—preachers who preach Jesus, preachers who preach a whole social gospel, and laywomen and laymen, like me, who navigate the currents of black thought between the two.

In fact, the controversy over the selected snippets of Wright's sermon has served to reemphasize the fullness, the multidimensionality of the black church.

It has underscored that its tradition encompasses not merely comforting the afflicted but also afflicting the comfortable. Not merely ratifying the status quo and the conventional wisdom, but instructing us, inspiring us to do things far beyond what we thought were the limits of our possibilities.

We are at one of those moments in history when millions of Americans have been inspired to think far beyond what, just recently, seemed to be the political limits of possibility.

Who would have thought it a possibility just a few years ago that a black man and a white woman would be competing for the presidential nomination of the Democratic Party?

As one born in 1935 in the Deep South who saw my father and oldest brother go off to Europe and Asia to fight in World War II and return home to Georgia unable by law to vote in the white primary, I stand here today—astonished, smashed, unbelieving, incredulous—that America has come to this place and time.

It is truly springtime in America.

But how did we get to this historic moment? Who planted the seeds that have brought forth this new fruit in our democracy?

Lest we forget that this event was brought about in part by the actions of men and women who at particular moments in time followed a deeply felt obligation to disturb the unjust peace and thereby advance the cause of justice.

Let me briefly cite examples—each of which is part of the long chain of events which have produced this singular moment in American political history.

Let us look beyond this year and back to a historic moment which gave women in America the right to vote for the first time in our history.

It began in 1776 when Abigail Adams wrote to her husband, John, attending the Continental Congress in Philadelphia and working on the Declaration of Independence.

She wrote, "Remember the ladies."

It fell on deaf ears because the declaration specifies that "all *men* are created equal."

In 1912, Theodore Roosevelt's Progressive Party becomes the first national political party to adopt a women's suffrage plank.

In 1916, Jeannette Rankin, of Montana, becomes the first American woman elected to the U.S. House of Representatives.

On August 26, 1920, the Nineteenth Amendment, called the Anthony Amendment, was ratified by one vote in the Tennessee legislature. That one vote cast to break the tie was by Henry Burn, a twenty-four-year-old antisuffragist whose mother instructed him to "remember the ladies."

Whatever your view of Hillary Clinton, she and her candidacy are the result of more than a century of work toward suffrage. Lest we forget that as Americans, regardless of party or preference, we should celebrate this milestone in our political process.

Further, as you contemplate Barack Obama's meteoric rise from a state senator in Illinois to a major contender for the Democratic nomination, whatever your view of him:

Read the 1947 U.S. District Court decision in *Elmore v. Rice*, which struck down the white primary in South Carolina.

Read the 1944 Supreme Court decision in *Smith v. Allright*, which struck down the white primary in Texas.

Read the 1945 U.S. District Court and the 1946 U.S. Circuit Court of Appeals decisions in *King v. Chatman*, which struck down the white primary in Georgia.

All of these cases were brought because blacks were denied the right to vote in the white primaries, which were controlled by state election officials and were tantamount to election.

These cases were brought by three black men who were disturbers of the unjust peace—George Elmore, Dr. Lonnie Smith, and Primus King. I met Dr. Lonnie Smith and I met George El-more, but I knew Primus King. Primus King was my man.

Born in 1900 in I latchechubbee, Alabama, the son of share-croppers, Primus E. King grew up in Columbus, Georgia, where his parents had moved to escape the grinding oppression of the sharecropping system. King was unlettered—like many South-ern blacks in those decades for whom the state and local govern-ments made formal schooling an impossibility.

But Primus King well understood the denial of rights blacks endured. His determination to be as independent as possible of the South's Jim Crow–rigged system of government and social relations showed itself early in his learning the trade of barbering. Later, in 1939, King's religious faith led him to become an itiner-ant Sunday preacher, ministering as called by one of the many small black churches that dotted the Black Belt countryside in Georgia and Alabama. It was that faith, he later said, which forti-fied him for the task he undertook on July 4, 1944.

On that day, Reverend Primus King walked into the Musco-gee County Courthouse in Columbus, Georgia, to cast his vote in the state's Democratic Party primary election. Because the racist Democratic Party monopolized political activity in Georgia as it did throughout the South, the primary determined the outcome of the general election. For that very reason, the state Democratic Party barred blacks from voting in the primary. It was that trav-esty of democracy that King, quietly supported by the local NAACP, intended to change.

"I am a citizen of this city and this state," he declared to the white election officials that day. "I own property. I pay taxes. I can read and write and do arithmetic, and I have not committed a crime of moral turpitude. I have come to vote."

His words got King roughly escorted out of the courthouse by police officers. But King persisted, and with the prearranged help of two local white lawyers, filed a federal suit to outlaw blacks' exclusion from the Democratic primary.

That brought a warning from party officials, who summoned King before them and bluntly told him that "If you don't withdraw the lawsuit, you could end up in the Chattahoochie River."

King, standing alone before the pillars of segregationist power, replied, "Well, if that happens, then at least I'll be thrown in the river for *something*, as opposed to all the colored people who've been thrown in there for *nothing*." And he walked out.

In October 1945, the Federal District Court in Macon, Georgia, ruled in King's favor, striking down the Georgia white primary. In March 1946, the U.S. Circuit Court of Appeals in New Orleans upheld that ruling, and the following month the U.S. Supreme Court declined to hear the Georgia Democratic Party's appeal.

The all-white Georgia Democratic primary now officially stood where it belonged—outside the bounds of the Constitution of the United States.

From George Elmore, Primus King, and Lonnie Smith to Barack Obama—lest we forget the journey.

And finally, it is a long way from the prisons of Vietnam, five and a half years of captivity, to the Republican nomination for president of the United States—lest we forget John McCain's journey, whatever our party affiliation or political differences.

Three Americans—a black, a woman, a senior citizen—contending for the highest office in the land. Let us be proud of this moment.

And lest we forget that moments like this are not happenstance: They are the direct result of the work, sacrifice, and passion of disturbers of the unjust peace.

And for the most part in our country, these disturbers of the unjust peace are unsung, unheralded, unknown, unappreciated. But they are our heroes.

Few have been honored with statues, parks, schools, stadiums, or academic chairs in their names.

But history honors them, and we honor them, and thank them.

Finally, I am reminded about the enduring value of something my mother taught me throughout her life.

As a youngster, when I made good grades, won declamation contests, was elected a class officer, had more than one girlfriend, I developed a little swagger. Acted a bit smug and cocky. My mother would take me aside and say, "Son, don't get too big for your britches." When I finished law school and won my first case, she warned, "Don't get too big for your britches." Until she could talk no more, that was her refrain.

Therefore, to you, to America, to the president and the Congress, to the world's greatest superpower ever, to my country with the mightiest economic, technological, and military forces the world has ever seen—to all the candidates, "Don't get too big for your britches."

The Babylonians, the Egyptians, and the Greeks of yore got "too big for their britches." The Roman Empire, which fell not from without but from within, got too big for its britches. Napoleon thought he would conquer the world, until in the hard cold of winter the Russians taught him that he "got too big for his britches." It was once said that the sun never set on the British Empire; now the sun has trouble finding the British Empire. Hitler, Mussolini, Stalin, and Saddam Hussein got "too big for their britches."

America's premier place in the world is not in fee simple absolute—the shining city on the hill is not ours in fee simple absolute. That Howard University is the capstone of black higher education is not ours in fee simple absolute. We earned it and must keep on earning it. We have come this far by faith and fight. Let us bow our heads:

> *God of our weary years,*
> *God of our silent tears,*
> *Thou who hast brought us thus far on the way;*
> *Thou who has by Thy might*
> *Led us into the light,*
> *Keep us forever in the path, we pray.*
> *Lest our feet stray from the places, our God, where we met Thee,*
> *Lest our hearts drunk with the wine of the world, we forget Thee;*
> *Shadowed beneath Thy hand,*
> *May we forever stand.*
> *True to our God,*
> *True to our native land.**

---

* James Weldon Johnson (1871–1938) wrote "Lift Every Voice and Sing" in 1900 for a celebration of Abraham Lincoln's birthday. It was published in *Saint Peter Relates an Incident: Selected Poems* (New York: Viking Press, 1935).

ACKNOWLEDGMENTS

Writing a book is a labor of love, and of a felt obligation, and, finally, of hope, too. The best one can ask for while enduring the moments that try one's patience and tests one's intellectual and physical reserves is to be surrounded by people as dedicated to the project's completion as you are. That has been my good fortune in working on this book. From the moment the idea sprouted, Peter Osnos, the founder and editor-at-large of PublicAffairs, Susan Weinberg, its publisher, and Clive Priddle, its executive editor, backed by their able, enthusiastic colleagues, directed a powerful stream of encouragement, practical advice, and subtle goading my way. Having benefited so greatly from their support of my first book, *Vernon Can Read!*, I expected no less—and I am immensely thankful to have been proved right. I benefited as well from the seasoned journalistic skills of Lee A. Daniels, who helped me recall the broader contemporary context of several of these speeches and made the writing of the commentary that accompanies them easier. I am also deeply grateful that I can continue to draw upon the skills and savviness of my assistants, Gayle Laughlin, at Akin, Gump, Strauss, Hauer & Feld in Washington, D.C., and Jeannie Adashek, at Lazard Frères & Co. in New York City. They are just two in number, but they constitute an entire army of support. Finally, words fail completely in describing the debt I owe my wife, Ann, for suffering me once again as I endured the arduous but ultimately satisfying endeavor of writing a book.

INDEX

Michael O'Neill

Vernon E. Jordan, Jr. is a senior managing director of Lazard Frères & Co. LLC and a senior counsel with Akin, Gump, Strauss, Hauer & Feld, LLP. Earlier in his career Mr. Jordan served as president and chief executive officer of the National Urban League, Inc.; executive director of the United Negro College Fund, Inc.; director of the Voter Education Project of the Southern Regional Council; attorney-consultant at the U.S. Office of Economic Opportunity; assistant to the executive director of the Southern Regional Council; Georgia field director of the National Association for the Advancement of Colored People; and as an attorney in private practice in Arkansas and Georgia. He is on the board of numerous companies and universities. He has been awarded more than sixty honorary degrees, and in 2001 was the recipient of the NAACP's highest honor, the Joel E. Spingarn Medal, awarded for distinguished achievement by black Americans. He is a graduate of DePauw University and the Howard University Law School, and is the author of *Vernon Can Read! A Memoir* (PublicAffairs, 2001).

PublicAffairs is a publishing house founded in 1997. It is a tribute to the standards, values, and flair of three persons who have served as mentors to countless reporters, writers, editors, and book people of all kinds, including me.

I. F. STONE, proprietor of *I. F. Stone's Weekly*, combined a commitment to the First Amendment with entrepreneurial zeal and reporting skill and became one of the great independent journalists in American history. At the age of eighty, Izzy published *The Trial of Socrates*, which was a national bestseller. He wrote the book after he taught himself ancient Greek.

BENJAMIN C. BRADLEE was for nearly thirty years the charismatic editorial leader of *The Washington Post*. It was Ben who gave the *Post* the range and courage to pursue such historic issues as Watergate. He supported his reporters with a tenacity that made them fearless and it is no accident that so many became authors of influential, best-selling books.

ROBERT L. BERNSTEIN, the chief executive of Random House for more than a quarter century, guided one of the nation's premier publishing houses. Bob was personally responsible for many books of political dissent and argument that challenged tyranny around the globe. He is also the founder and longtime chair of Human Rights Watch, one of the most respected human rights organizations in the world.

•   •   •

For fifty years, the banner of Public Affairs Press was carried by its owner Morris B. Schnapper, who published Gandhi, Nasser, Toynbee, Truman, and about 1,500 other authors. In 1983, Schnapper was described by *The Washington Post* as "a redoubtable gadfly." His legacy will endure in the books to come.

Peter Osnos, *Founder and Editor-at-Large*

CPSIA information can be obtained at www.ICGtesting.com
Printed in the USA
LVOW06s1151011015

456493LV00003B/15/P